COME AND SEE!

COME AND SEE!

A Lent journey for Adults,
Young People and Children
using individual study
and all-age activities

SUSAN SAYERS

Drawings by Arthur Baker,
Helen Herbert, Roy Mitchell

First published 1990
in Great Britain by
KEVIN MAYHEW LTD
Rattlesden
Bury St Edmunds, Suffolk IP30 0SZ

ISBN 0 86209 171 3

Cover by Lyn Ellis
Typesetting by John Liffen, Ipswich, Suffolk
Printed and bound in Great Britain by
Southampton Book Co. Ltd.

CONTENTS

INTRODUCTION

THIS is a Lent course with a difference. Many parishes have already begun to enjoy the move towards all-age worship; others are interested but sceptical about practicalities. This course provides an opportunity for Christians of all ages to walk quite a challenging route through Lent. Each day of the week, different age bands will follow the route at their own level, and once a week there is a shared session called 'Together in Christ', during which all the ideas of the week come together, and those in each age band will find themselves able to contribute and help others.

The course should work just as well with a family or small group of friends as with larger parishes and ecumenical groups, and the need for leadership and organisation has been deliberately kept to a minimum, so that groups will be able to organise themselves. All that is needed is to arrange a time and meeting place each week, and for one person in each group to pick the hymns or choruses from the suggestion list, and have the words available.

'Come and See!' is what Philip said to Nathanael, and this course is a journey to meet the living Christ, getting to know him better, and allowing him to work in our lives, both as individuals and as the Church. In a sense it is a spiral course. As we travel, we will find we are covering similar ground but at a deeper level and from a different angle. What we have discovered earlier will help us to make sense of the new material. Each person will need daily access to a Bible and a course book. Children will also need art and craft materials such as felt tip pens, scissors and glue.

Every Saturday is research/activity day, with suggestions for further study, along with model-making for children. Younger children (under seven years) will need some help with their activities.

Each day's study is split into three broad age bands:

Mainly for adults	(18+)
Mainly for young people	(13-17)
Mainly for children	(5-12)

Do feel free to follow whichever suits you best – there are no rigid cut-off points. I suggest that you glance through all the sections for the first day or two before deciding definitely. Some of you may find it helps to follow one band, but to read the others as well if you have time, or would like another angle on the day's study.

Each day's programme consists of a Bible reading, a section to set you thinking about what you have read and how it applies to you, and an exercise to do during the day. The aim is that you end up closer to the Lord, knowing and loving him more deeply; more aware of his love for you, and the remarkable changes he can make in your life.

Suggestions for songs and choruses have been made from the following sources:

Alleluia!
Come and Praise
Ishmael Praise Party
MSOTS (More Songs of the Spirit)
OANA (Hymns Old & New, Anglican edition)
SOF (Songs of Fellowship)
SOF4 (Songs of Fellowship, 4)

ASH WEDNESDAY FOR ADULTS

WEEK ONE
WHERE CAN WE FIND HIM?

OPENING UP

Read John 1:43-46

This may not seem a very promising start to our search for Jesus. Although Philip is falling over his words in his excitement, Nathanael, like many of us, is far more sceptical. His reply, 'Can anything good come out of Nazareth?' is just the kind of comment many of us might make. For Nathanael, to find the Messiah came from Nazareth was about as likely as us bumping into the Queen pushing her shopping trolley in our local supermarket. Or, to put it another way, how would you react if your friend came and told you the Messiah, whom you had waited and longed for, hailed from somewhere like Salford or Clapham? Pleasant as Salford, Clapham and Nazareth may be, they are not renowned cities like Rome, London or Jerusalem.

We use our experiences to make sense of life, and fix it in patterns to tame it and keep it in our control. This is an important survival strategy, and shows an intelligent animal. But we can take it too far. If our lives jog along in the same pattern too long, we lose the flexibility of pioneers and no longer walk with our eyes alerted for unusual or surprising events. The pattern we have fitted life into seems to fit so snugly that we don't feel the need to adjust it to new circumstances. We can even get to the point where, if the circumstances don't fit our pattern, we start assuming that the circumstances must be wrong because we *know* our pattern is right!

In such stiffness, God must find us so hard to move. We need to have the oil of expectancy poured into our stiff joints so that we are able to move again spiritually with as much agility as when we were exploring the world as children.

To do today

Wherever you go today, and in whatever you are doing, imagine you are there for the first time. Notice everything as if you have never seen, heard, touched, tasted or smelt it before.

OPENING UP
Read John 1:43-46

Have you ever noticed how quickly gossip can spread? Something you tell a couple of friends in strict secrecy one evening can be all over the school by the following afternoon! If you could colour the gossip fluorescent green, it would be interesting to watch it spreading outwards, something like this:

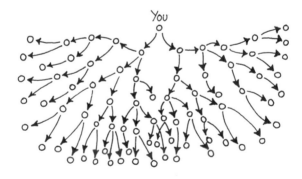

See what power you have!

Now think of all the times something boring has been up on a notice board. Hardly anyone remembers it, do they? In fact, I've sometimes thought that the best way to keep a secret would be to put it on a typed A4 sheet of paper on a notice board.

Jesus went for the gossip approach. When he collected those he wanted to work with him he didn't put out official ads. Instead, the pattern went a bit like this, according to John:

FIRST he called: Peter and Andrew (who were brothers).

SECOND he called: Philip (who lived in the same town).

THIRD Philip brought along Nathanael (Philip's friend).

Jesus sometimes does the same thing now. If one person suddenly meets Jesus and realises he is real and alive, and can do incredible things in someone's life, then that person will start talking excitedly, and the news will spread. People get interested when something real, alive and powerful is going on. They start wanting to know more. It could be that Jesus is choosing you to be the first person in your school, college, home or place of work.

To do today

At every odd time you remember – change of lessons, in the bus queue, in the bathroom – tell Jesus, in your own ordinary words, that you would like to find out more about him and get to know him. EXPECT him to take you up on this.

OPENING UP

Draw these in the right places

If you had lost this where would you look for it?

If you wanted this where would you go to get it?

If you needed this where would you find it?

We are going to look for Jesus.
This is what you will need to bring:-

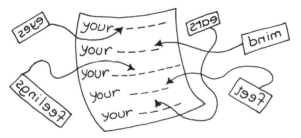

*Look in a mirror to find them!

To do today

Put a tick beside each thing on the list that you use today. If you use it a lot, put *two* ticks.

COME AND SEE

Read John 1:46-51

This time we start with Nathanael's doubts, and see how Philip uses them. If he had tried to explain more about Jesus at this point, before Nathanael had met Jesus, his words may not have meant much. Anyway, why try to explain running water to someone when you can turn on the tap? So Philip invites Nathanael to make up his mind on his own experience of Jesus – 'Come and see,' he says.

Sometimes we can put people off by talking about Jesus instead of simply inviting them to come and see. Perhaps we have been put off ourselves by language which doesn't mean much to us, or by an impression of Jesus given to us which doesn't seem terribly relevant to our own way of living. Perhaps we know a lot about Jesus, but have never felt we have actually met him in person. Maybe we feel it is arrogant to expect to do so before death.

But forget normal time for a moment. For God, a thousand years is no more than a day. So, in a sense, the resurrection happened less than two days ago! I mention this, not to tie ourselves down to literal fundamentalism, but just to get our minds sharpened again to the reality of Jesus being fully alive. He is as freshly alive for us today as he was for the women at the empty tomb, and the disciples in the upper room behind locked doors. All we need to do to find him is to seek him, because he has promised us that everyone – not just 'the first lucky thousand' – who seeks will find.

Notice how, when Nathanael comes to find Jesus,

Jesus knows him already! That knocks Nathanael for six. Those who know us before we know them, even on a superficial level, can sometimes fill us with dread and apprehension. After all, we all have things in our past that we would prefer people *not* to know! And Nathanael senses that Jesus knows him in a very deep way. But it is Jesus' loving nature to be gentle with us. He encourages and reassures Nathanael straight away by appreciating the goodness in him. He will do the same with us.

To do today

Keep your eyes (and hearts) open to see the good in every person you meet during the day.

COME AND SEE
Read John 1:46-51

It may be that you felt a bit of a fool yesterday, telling Jesus you wanted to get to know him better. It is difficult to talk to someone you can't see, and don't know very well yet – a bit like talking on the phone before the other person has picked up the receiver. How can you be sure he's there, even?

Well, at the moment, perhaps you can't, and I would be cheating you if I tried to persuade you otherwise. I would like you to take my word for it for a short while, along with the word of the millions who, through the centuries, have discovered that Jesus is alive, well and living in their neighbourhood. But don't worry about it – if you have been telling him you want to know him better, sooner or later he will certainly make his presence known.

Look at what happened to this person Nathanael, who started to look for Jesus without much hope that he'd really find anyone important. After all, Jesus only came from a very ordinary town down the road. But still, he went to look for him. And that's what you're doing, and in many ways it's the most important brave thing you've ever done in your life. Because if you're really going to meet the person who made the solar system, your toenails, cocoa beans and that strange substance which you can swim in, wash with, drink or skate on, then there's no way you'll carry on being the same as you are now when you've met him!

If the thought of that kind of power is beginning to make you feel a little wary of going further, then that's great. It means you are already beginning to know something of God's tremendous potency. He's much too powerful for you to control. What's more, he already knows you, both by name and character: not image – not what you want people to see you as – Jesus knows you as you really are.

Does that sound like bad news? Yes, I agree, if he had all that power and no love, it would be very bad news indeed. But look at how he welcomes Nathanael, picking out his good points and delighted that he has come. That's how he welcomes you, too.

To do today

Look out for things God has made which show his power, and make a list of them.

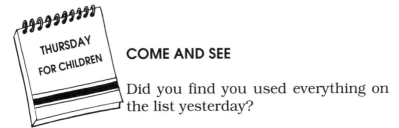

COME AND SEE

Did you find you used everything on the list yesterday?

No wonder we need to rest at night – our bodies and minds are working all the time!

Who is your best friend?_____

Draw a picture of
your best friend here.

What do you
like playing together? _____

When we have some good news, we like telling our friends about it, don't we? Well, when Philip met Jesus, he went straight to his friend, Nathanael, and told him all about it.

'Listen, Nat,' said Philip. 'You know Moses and the prophets always promised that one day God would send a very special leader to us?'

'Yes, I know,' said Nat. 'What about it?'

'Well, he's here! We've met him!' said Philip. He was hopping about with excitement. Nathanael's eyes opened wide. 'You mean you've met the one we've all been waiting for? You mean he's really come?'

'I'm sure of it,' Philip said, nodding his head. 'His name is Jesus and he comes from Nazareth.'

'Huh! Can anything good come out of Nazareth?' grunted Nat.

Philip looked at his friend. What on earth could he say to make Nat believe him? Suddenly he had an idea. He needn't tell Nat anything else – he would just drag his friend along to meet Jesus for himself. Once he had actually met Jesus, Philip knew Nat would understand.

'Just you come and see!' he grinned.

'O.K. Philip, I'll come!' agreed Nat. And together they set off to find Jesus.

Jesus saw them coming. Being Jesus, he could tell a lot about Nat just by looking at him, and he obviously loved what he saw. As Nat came towards him he said to the others, 'Now here is a real Israelite coming – there's certainly nothing false in him! . . . Oh, hello Nathanael, welcome!'

Nat looked from Jesus to Philip and back to Jesus again. Philip was grinning again. He had so wanted his friend and Jesus to meet. Nat's mouth was still gaping. 'H.. how do you know me?' he asked Jesus. Jesus looked right into him again. Not with the kind of look that makes you squirm and feel guilty. This look made Nat feel really loved and understood. It made him feel happy.

'Oh,' Jesus was saying, 'I saw you when you were under the fig tree.' Nat thought fast. So Jesus must have known him and waited for him to come, even before Philip invited him. That wasn't possible, surely!

Jesus seemed to know what Nat was thinking. 'Yes.' he said quietly, 'I saw you before Philip called you.' That did it. Nat knelt down right there in the dust. He realised Philip had been right about this man. 'Teacher!' he said happily, 'You are the Son of God! You are the King of Israel!'

Jesus laughed kindly. 'Do you believe just because I told you I saw you when you were under the fig tree? You will see greater things than this, you know.'

Nat, for the moment, didn't care too much about the future. He just knew that being with Jesus felt wonderful, and nothing would ever be ordinary again.

To do today

Whenever you remember, all through the day, tell Jesus you would like to come and meet him as well.

RECOGNISING HIS PRESENCE
Read Luke 10:23-24

Did you find that you were surprised by the amount of goodness you noticed during the last exercise? Very often we become immunised against seeing good in the ordinary, daily events of our life, and we are much sharper at seeing the niggles and grumps around us. Try making that exercise a regular habit, and refuse to let your spiritual eyesight become myopic. 'Heaven and earth are full of your glory,' we sing in the Gloria. If we open our eyes expecting to see some of that glory, we shall find it, often in the most surprising people and places!

In today's reading, the seventy-two disciples whom Jesus had sent out in two's have just come back, excited, and hardly able to believe the amazing healings they have carried out in Jesus' name. You can imagine them all swapping stories and dying to tell Jesus all about it.

In this 'pre-run' of the world-wide spread of the church, we can recognise the same kind of joy and amazement that occurs today whenever Christians suddenly find that Jesus really can work wonders in their lives, and in the lives of those for whom they pray.

Jesus shares the excitement of his returning disciples and joins in all the rejoicing. And, seeing with eyes of eternity, his joy in the present alerts him to think of all those in the past who longed to see the kingdom of heaven so close, but lived too early to witness it. There were also plenty living at the time who saw, but did not notice.

So, if we want to meet Jesus, we have to expect to find him. You have seen for yourself that there is more goodness around than we normally notice. It's a bit like looking through different coloured toffee wrappers – if you look through purple, you can only see purple; if you look through yellow you can't see anything white. If we look at life as if it is entirely material and ordinary, we shall be quite unable to see all the glory of the extraordinary which is there. But if we look at life expecting to see there God, alive and real, much will surprise us with joy.

Where are we going, then, in our search to find Jesus? Well, we have all the events of the Gospels to explore, and all the longings of those prophets and kings. We have the world itself and every part of creation including the human element. And we have the living, risen Christ himself whom, through the Holy Spirit of God, we are enabled to meet in person. Quite an agenda. All we need for this journey of discovery – open eyes, open hearts and open minds. Let's begin straight away.

To do today

Make a chart of all the factors which have helped you to find out what God is like.

People	Places	Events	Things

RECOGNISING HIS PRESENCE
Read Luke 10:23-24

Yesterday we were noticing the power of God as it shows in everything around us. Those prophets and kings Jesus talks about in today's reading did the same thing, and learnt a lot about God in the process. But however much you've heard about a favourite group, say, or seen photos of them, or heard tracks from their best albums, there's nothing to beat actually meeting them.

Meeting Jesus is meeting God with a human face, and those living in Galilee during the Roman occupation there nearly two thousand years ago, were able to sit down under the same tree and talk with Jesus, and walk along beside him enjoying his company. They could stand nearby and watch people who had been blind for years suddenly receive their sight again. They would have seen withered hands straightening out before their eyes.

At one point, Jesus sent seventy-two of them out in two's to the villages he would soon be visiting. They found that, working in Jesus' name, they too could heal people, talk with them powerfully and get rid of evil and disease. They came back thrilled to be part of all this positive power and liberation that Jesus had started. That's when Jesus, who was just as excited as they were, remembered all those who had lived too early to see it all.

What about us? We're a bit like prophets and kings, and a bit like Jesus' contemporaries. After all, just as the prophets lived too early to see Jesus in Nazareth, we live too late to be part of the crowd hearing him teach from a fishing boat, or squashed in the doorway of a house with all the other sweaty bodies, watching the sick made well. But, thanks to the gospel writers, we do know quite a lot of what went on, and can imagine being there.

That's not all. Jesus, unlike any other person ever, is not tied to being alive in a particular place at a particular time. Time travelling, Dr Who or Back to the Future style, picks up on what we'd all love to do. Wouldn't it be great if we could set out on our programmed time vehicle and watch Jesus at work. I wonder what he would say to us? And who would you bring for him to touch and heal?

Well, the day-dreaming is nice, but the truth is even better, and far more practical. Since the resurrection, Jesus is able to walk straight into our lives in our time, speaking our language and fully aware of everything in our society and culture. The same goes for every person wherever they are and whenever they live. That is possible, because Jesus is Lord – in charge, and unlimited by the time/space barriers we have as human beings.

To do today

If Jesus walked into your town this week . . . what do you think would happen? Would you offer him accommodation or direct him on somewhere else? Who would he spend time with, do you think?

RECOGNISING HIS PRESENCE (GETTING TO KNOW HIM)

Yesterday you were telling Jesus you would like to meet him yourself. He loves hearing about you, as well. As you fill in this chart, do it for Jesus. You won't need to send it – while you are writing it, he will be receiving it.

Dear Jesus,

My name is_____ and

I am_____years old.

This is what I look like:

My favourite colour is _____

and the food I like best is

_____

What I enjoy doing is

_____

What makes me happy is

_____

What makes me sad is_____

What I like best in your world is/are _____

_____

With love from

_____

23

TO DO TODAY

Look at these ideas about what praying is.

Use some of them today!

RESEARCH DAY

Gradually the truth of God's saving love is unfolded and revealed to us. Look up and read each of these references to get a glimpse of how this happened. Don't panic – each one is very short! Genesis 12:2-3; Psalm 108:4; 2 Samuel 7:16; Psalm 118:22; Isaiah 7:13-14; Isaiah 11:1-2; Micah 5:2-4; Zechariah 9:9.

RESEARCH DAY

Fit the words into the right spaces.

Ben Hur   origin   Kings   people

Encyclopedia Brittanica   The Complete Works of Shakespeare   Psalms

Chronicles

Samuel   Genesis   Exodus   The Bible

★ The world's best-selling book is ☐☐☐ ☐☐☐☐☐

★ The word Genesis means ☐☐☐☐☐☐ and tells about the beginning of our universe, and the way God works with the people he has created.

★ The book of ☐☐☐☐☐☐ is a hymn book and a prayer book, collected for worship by the people of Israel.

★ The books of ☐☐☐☐☐☐☐☐☐ mainly cover the same historical events as the books of ☐☐☐☐☐ and ☐☐☐☐☐, but from the priests' point of view.

ACTIVITY DAY

Make a secret box of delights!
Today you are going to make something which looks very dull and ordinary from the outside. But when you take the trouble to look carefully, you'll find all kinds of surprises!

You will need:
* a cardboard box with a lid (like a shoe box)
* scissors
* sticky tape
* tissue paper
* thin card
* glue
* paints, felt tips, bright coloured paper foil etc.

See the next page for what to do.

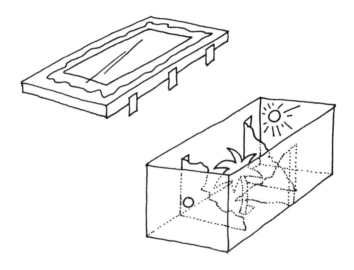

Tape the lid to the box
when you have finished.

1. Cut a hole in the lid and cover it with tissue paper.
2. Cut a peep hole in one end of the box.
3. Cut shapes from thin card to stick into the box like pieces of scenery in a theatre. Decorate the whole box inside to look like a beautiful place – under the sea, in a jungle, among snowy mountains, or anywhere else you like. Use plenty of bright colours and enjoy yourself! Bring your secret box to the 'Together in Christ' session, so everyone there can enjoy it too.

TOGETHER IN CHRIST 1

Part 1

First, have a look at what the children have made – sit in a circle and let the children bring round their boxes. Enjoy the boxes, finding out from the children how they made them and which bits they liked doing best.

Sing together now. If you have someone to accompany you, that's fine, but it certainly doesn't matter if you haven't. The important thing as far as God is concerned, is that you all MEAN what you sing! Sing the choruses through several times, if you like.

Seek ye first (OANA 445)

Open our eyes, Lord (OANA 386)

Pray together, aloud or in silence, for the Lord to teach you and show you more of himself. Don't forget to pray expectantly.

Part 2

Pair up with someone of a different age group who you don't know too well. You have five minutes to find out all you can about your partner. Just one rule – treat one another with love and respect! When time is up, hold hands in a circle and sing *Bind us together, Lord* (OANA 47).

Part 3

Get into mixed groups of 3-6, to discuss these questions:

1. How did Nathanael hear about Jesus?
2. Why did Philip want him to meet Jesus?
3. What do we need to have if we want to meet Jesus?
4. What can we find in the Old and New Testaments that lead us to him?
5. How else can we find him?
6. How have you been surprised by God recently?

Part 4

Come together now to praise God and thank him for giving us Jesus. Ideas for hymns/choruses:

   Jubilate everybody (OANA 274)

   Shine, Jesus, shine (SOF4 110)

   Oh how good is the Lord (OANA 364)

and finish with a shared hug of peace – everyone exchanging the peace with everyone else.

WEEK TWO
WHAT IS HE DOING?

CHANGING LIVES
Read Luke 19:1-10

Jesus' ministry among his contemporaries was really quite short – probably two or three years. What was he doing during that time which changed so many lives so dramatically then, and still stirs up new life in so many today? All great times of spiritual revival have grown from people looking closely and imaginatively at the written records we have of those years. So much so, that it seems the obvious place for us to explore.

Let's start with watching the way Zacchaeus changes through meeting Jesus personally. Obviously he (like us on this course) is looking for an opportunity to catch sight of Jesus. Also, perhaps like us, he would prefer to get a good look at Jesus from a distance before actually committing himself to anything he may later regret! Being a chief tax collector and rich, suggests that Zacchaeus was well used to looking for unofficial ways to get what he wanted. Today in Jericho he quickly assesses the situation, gives up on getting through the crowd, and instead runs on ahead to climb the sycamore before anyone else gets there.

Jesus recognises that Zacchaeus has made an effort to see him, so he builds on that quality of single-mindedness and redirects it. He gives him something else to be single-minded about – entertaining Jesus at his home; looking after someone else's comfort for a change. And the result is that

Zacchaeus, never a man to do things by halves, puts right all his past wrongs, paying people back with the kind of rate of interest he had possibly been charging them, regardless of whether they could afford it or not.

So, when Jesus meets someone who is seeking him out, he does not condemn, no matter what is lurking in their past. Nor does he expect or want them to be different. He enjoys and appreciates the qualities and characteristics they possess, even if these have caused them to sin. (Think of the woman caught in the act of adultery.) And so it is with us. Whatever characteristics, weaknesses and habits we have, Jesus loves us with them all included. Although our encounter with him will change us, it won't sap us of our colour. Far from it.

Suppose you have a tendency to gossip – Jesus may use you to be a spreader of his good news in words ordinary people can understand in a natural way. Suppose you tend to get into habits that are hard to break – Jesus may well change your tobacco/alcohol dependency to a God dependency, which you will enjoy far more and is far better for your health!

Don't feel you have got to put your best self on before you are ready to meet Jesus. Don't feel you've got to wait until you have fewer doubts about him, or until you've sorted out a bad relationship, or until you've conquered your nastiest habits.

The evidence of the gospels shows that Jesus loves meeting people right where they are, in the mess of their lives, with their teeth unbrushed and their jobs unfinished. He liberates them by re-aligning and enhancing what they already are.

To do today

Learn by heart the last verse of today's reading – Luke 19:10.

CHANGING LIVES

Read Luke 19:1-10

Jews thought of the tax collectors as scum. They considered them traitors because they worked for the Romans, and the Romans were disliked because they were a foreign power occupying the Jews' country. You can imagine that anyone collecting taxes for an occupying ruler would be despised – especially since the taxes were very high. Added to this, you could make quite a bit of money on the side as a tax collector. How? You just charged people even more than the official Roman amount and pocketed the difference. It's very likely that Zacchaeus had made his fortune that way.

With his sharp eye for getting what he wants, Zacchaeus leaves the shoving crowd and shins up a sycamore tree further along the road. Now he'll have the best view and no hassle. The people would expect Jesus to ignore Zacchaeus with the contempt they reckon he deserves, but Jesus talks to him as if he's known him for ages, and is already a firm friend. The way he talks to him, and uses his name, sounds as if he actually likes him.

You know how it feels when someone you're interested in actually comes across and talks to you? Doesn't it feel great! I bet Zacchaeus felt at least 5 centimetres taller. Never mind the shocked whispers of the crowd – Zacchaeus has Jesus as a friend, and his self esteem has lift-off.

As a result of all this, Zacchaeus is turned inside out, really. Instead of charging people fantastically high interest on their taxes, he's now dishing out fantastically high rates of compensation. Jesus has somehow managed to make Zacchaeus use his natural characteristics positively for good, instead of negatively for self-gain and others' distress.

We've just looked at the effect on one person, but the gospels are crowded with others who, as a result of knowing Jesus, have their lives changed and set free. This meeting and loving to wholeness was a big part of what Jesus was doing on earth. He still does it now, and the pattern is the same – anyone who takes the trouble to see him is welcomed and accepted with friendship, and often humour and directness. He never waffles on, he gets straight to the point and leads us to whatever next step is right for us. And it doesn't matter to Jesus what mess we're in when we go to find him, because he's in the business of working from where we are now. He knows all about us, and why we are as we are. His saving love is not a pre-packaged deal of a rough size to suit every customer. His way is to present us with a personalised, individually-styled salvation, which fits us perfectly, because to him, at any one time, YOU are the most special person there is. And it's the same for everyone else, too!

To do today

Make a list of any people you have forgotten to repay, decided to ignore or made life unpleasant for.
FIRST tell Jesus their names.
SECOND ask him to help you put things right.
THIRD use the opportunities he will give you to do just that.
FOURTH tell Jesus what you've done. I needn't tell you to thank him – you'll be amazed how thankful and relieved you feel.

CHANGING LIVES

Have you ever climbed a tree? How would you climb this one?

When you are not very tall, all you can see in a crowded shop is baskets and legs, isn't it! If you want to see better in a crowd, what do you do?

climb on Dad's shoulders?

Squeeze through the legs to the front of the crowd?

climb on a wall?

Well, Zacchaeus was not very tall, and he went and climbed a tree so he could see Jesus. Soon the crowd following Jesus got to Zacchaeus' tree. Jesus stopped. He looked up at Zacchaeus, perched in the tree like a large bird, and called to him. 'Hurry up and come down, Zacchaeus!' said Jesus. 'I'm coming to stay at your house today.' You could hear the crowds were horrified. Zacchaeus had cheated people out of their money; he worked for the Romans. He wasn't worth Jesus talking to, let alone staying with. Fancy Jesus choosing him! They muttered and grumbled under their breath.

Of course Zac was tickled pink. He shot down that tree so fast, he nearly ripped his coat. 'Certainly, Jesus . . . it's just down this street . . . do you like pomegranates? . . . Make way for Jesus everyone! . . .'

I don't know what Zacchaeus and Jesus talked

about that day, but whatever it was made Zac want to change his life. 'I'm going to give back twice as much as I've borrowed from everyone,' he announced. 'And if I've taken money from them, I'll pay them back four times as much!'

The people looked at one another in amazement. This wasn't mean old Zac talking, was it? Jesus was very pleased about it. He knew that although Zacchaeus wouldn't be so rich living like this, he would be free and happy.

To do today

Do something kind and friendly for someone you don't usually help much.

HEALING
Read Luke 5:17-26

Another big area of Jesus' work is healing, so today we are watching how he deals with a paralysed man. Once again, notice the effort made by those friends to get to Jesus. If we are really determined to do something, it shows in the lengths we are prepared to go to in order to achieve it. It's no good kidding ourselves we're seeking Jesus purposefully if in fact we fit this in as a noble little 'extra' in our busy, important schedules. It has to come first, not last.

Notice how Jesus always picks out and appreciates the good intentions and efforts of those who come looking for him, however unconventional their methods and routes. Notice, too, how he always starts from where they are. When Jesus looks at the man whose friends are determined to help, he sees a man whose distress is caused not so much by his physical paralysis as by a deep, uncontrollable guilt, which is making his whole life a misery. Perhaps the man blames himself for some event in the past – possibly the shame he feels he has caused his parents by being paralysed – and the agony of living with this self-destructive burden has paralysed his spirit to match his body.

Jesus sees, understands and immediately responds to provide what will bring the man freedom. He speaks to him as a loving, friendly parent; words of forgiveness spoken with such authority that they cut through the man's self-doubt and assure even him of their truth. This was the healing the man needed. Its effectiveness must have shown clearly to his friends and many of the by-standers. Perhaps he was laughing, as the newfound lightness made him suddenly aware of the humour of the situation – sitting under a gaping hole in someone else's house with everyone staring! Certainly he would not now see everything so heavily and could delight in a sense of the ridiculous.

This healing brings to light the need for healing in others. Up to the surface squirm jealousy, small-mindedness and resentment among some of those witnessing the man's freedom. Immediately Jesus addresses their need, starting where they are by speaking to calm and reassure their fears. It will help them, as well as the man, if physical healing happens, to match and 'authenticate' the spiritual healing. So, when Jesus tells the man to take up his mat and walk home, he is offering healing both to the man himself and also to those crippled by jealousy, or anxiety about accepting Jesus as God's chosen one.

Those who are receptive (including the freshly forgiven paralysed man) are cured. In some, the seeds of faith have been sown; in others, rejection blocks their healing.

To do today

When you come before the Lord today, ask him to show you what needs healing in you. Be prepared for a frustrating day, because he may well show you, by allowing you to see your jealousy/resentment/impatience/irritability/ambition etc. in action! When you find yourself reacting with powerful inner anger, remember what you asked for, and learn from what you have been shown. Now you are in a much better position to be healed, and can ask for healing.

HEALING

Read Luke 5:17-26

We saw yesterday what a powerful impact Jesus has on people who spend time in his company. Did you get round to doing the exercise yesterday? If you did, you will have experienced the same lightness and freedom which Zacchaeus felt. If you haven't done the exercise yet, it isn't too late – take a deep breath and plunge into it today. I know it's hard but you won't regret it!

Some of those Jesus met on earth were ill, so today we're looking at how Jesus reacts to illness. This paralysed man seems to have some fantastic friends, and, judging by the trouble they're taking to get the man to Jesus, they are convinced that Jesus will be able to set their friend's body free to move normally. Lots of the healings in the gospels are to do with setting people free.

Jesus takes one look at the man, and realises that the main problem here isn't in the crippled body but in the mind and heart. Jesus can see how some guilt is gnawing away at the man inside him, making him unable to enjoy his life and his friends or anything else, for that matter. We don't know why he feels guilty, and Jesus is not the kind of person who would blurt it out in front of a crowd – he never shows anyone up like that. But his look tells the man that he knows the score and understands. It's a private matter between the two of them.

Have you ever been messing about in class while a teacher no one respects is getting hot under the collar telling you all off, and no one takes a blind bit of notice? Then perhaps another member of staff comes along who everyone does respect. They only have to say one word, or raise their eyebrows and that's enough to quell the riot and settle you all down.

Well, that is the kind of authority Jesus has. So when he tells the man that his sins are forgiven, there isn't any doubt about it – they really are, and the man knows it. His body may still be paralysed, but he feels over the moon!

It's interesting how this affects the Pharisees. 'Good heavens,' they're thinking, 'He sounds like God almighty!' (or thought-balloons to that effect). The man who's just been freed from his guilt knows they're very near the truth. But because they aren't expecting the Messiah to act in the way Jesus is acting, they see Jesus as an upstart who's getting too big for his boots.

So Jesus gives them another clue to his identity by showing authority over the man's crippled body, loosening it all, so that the man can just stand up, roll up his sleeping mat, and walk home like anyone else. Now wouldn't you think that this would get the Pharisees suspecting great things of Jesus? Who on earth can this man be?

Those who are open-minded and open-hearted, are filled with excitement, wonder and fear all mixed up, because they know they are standing next to someone with extraordinary power and love, similar to what they know God possesses. Those who are narrow-minded still can't see the good news, even though it is staring them in the face.

To do today

1. If there's any 'business' outstanding from yesterday, do it today.
2. Think of a person or a situation who/which is sick and needs healing. In your imagination, bring them through the crowd somehow until you can lay them down at Jesus' feet. Now ask him to heal them, and trust that he will do so in the best possible way.

HEALING

Can you remember being ill? What was the matter with you?

Look at the next page and . . .

. . . tick the list about how you felt:

	YES	NO
tired		
hot		
cold		
grumpy		
sore		
sad		
lonely		
fed up		

When we are feeling very ill, all we want is to feel better again! Jesus knew that, and whenever he met anyone who was ill, he enjoyed making them feel completely well – better than they had ever been before.

Read about how Jesus healed a man who couldn't walk. It's in the gospel of Luke, chapter 5, verses 17 to 26. Then see if you can put these parts of the story in the right order.

1. So they made a hole in the roof.

2. Some men wanted Jesus to heal their friend who was paralysed.

3. Jesus told him his sins were forgiven.

4. There were so many crowds that they couldn't reach Jesus through the door.

5. Full of joy, the man found he could walk!

6. Then he said, 'Pick up your mat and walk home!'

7. They let the man down through the hole to the feet of Jesus.

Put the numbers in the right order in the boxes:

To do today

Imagine Jesus sitting and talking to a crowd of people and healing them. Think of someone you know who needs healing or help. Hold their hand (or carry them if they are little) and bring them to Jesus. Ask him to make them better, and trust him to do this in the best way.

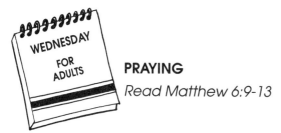

PRAYING

Read Matthew 6:9-13

Yesterday we saw an extraordinary power at work in Jesus for the freeing and healing of humanity. Jesus could not bear to leave people lost and suffering, and his great love for each person as being 'special' was time and again translated into practical acts of healing them to wholeness. This was not without cost. We know ourselves how tired and drained we get after spending time helping someone we love through a crisis of some kind. For Jesus, too, the healing was truly *work* of love, and he must often have become exhausted after expending so much all day, as the stream of trusting, hopeful, desperate men, women and children struggled to him in great need.

Whenever Jesus healed them, he felt power go out of him. That's how he knew the woman with severe bleeding had been healed. But Jesus was not a workaholic, and knew how vital it was to have periods of time alone with God his Father. So he was always disappearing off into the hills to pray, often late at night or very early in the morning. Sometimes he would spend whole nights in prayer. These were not times of duty, but of deep, refreshing communion which enabled him to cope with the work of the day.

The disciples realised the importance of these times to Jesus, and they also saw the effectiveness of them in Jesus' life and actions. This made them eager to know more about the way Jesus prayed, so they asked him to teach them how it was done. It may be helpful, first, to look at what he *didn't* tell them.

He didn't give specific times or positions to use. He didn't give them a long lecture on how they should do it. Instead, he used clear, simple phrases which cannot be said sincerely without checking our attitude towards God and towards one another. As soon as we begin to call God 'our Father' we are placed in his presence as brothers and sisters together – sons and daughters of our creator. As soon as we pray for forgiveness in the same measure as we forgive those who have sinned against us, we are thrown headlong into the practical business of putting things right in our relationships and acknowledging our need of God's loving power in our lives. All through the Lord's Prayer we are being gently and steadily transformed into new creatures, with hearts of stone being melted into hearts of flesh, which can spread the warmth of God's love out into a weary and often disillusioned world.

To do today

Pray the Lord's Prayer over the space of about half an hour, taking one phrase at a time, and immersing yourself in what it means, how it challenges you, how it encourages and how it deepens your relationship with God.

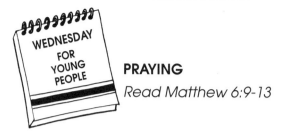

PRAYING

Read Matthew 6:9-13

So far this week we have found Jesus very involved with people – meeting and talking with them, changing their lives, freeing them from guilt and from illness. Today we are going to look at how he spends his time when he is alone.

When you haven't got anything particular to do, what does your mind usually settle to thinking about? A particular person, perhaps? Something you are really looking forward to? Something you wish could happen? Those kinds of daydreams are useful because they point to where your real 'treasure' is in life. You may think you have decided what treasure your life is founded on, but in fact, your life is built on whatever you spend most time thinking about. Quite a thought, isn't it! Do we want our whole life to be built on clothes or a holiday, or even the latest boy/girlfriend?

It's great to enjoy all those things, and I'm sure God delights in us enjoying what he has made. But when they get to the stage of occupying your mind and heart whenever possible, they have really become gods, and what you are doing is worshipping them. Worshipping idols doesn't mean bowing down before your favourite tape and saying, 'O tape, I adore you!', any more than worshipping God necessarily means kneeling down and rattling off set prayers which might bypass your mind and heart.

What's all this got to do with Jesus being alone? Well, when he was able to have quiet times (he made time by nipping out to the hills in the late evening or

very early morning) he spent his time in the company of his 'treasure' – God his Father. If I call it
praying, I don't want you get the wrong idea of what
was going on. He wasn't necessarily 'saying prayers',
though no doubt the psalms and prayers he knew
would come into it.

But really, for him, praying was spending time in
God's company, with all his being – his mind, his
heart, his body – all attuned to God, whether in
silence, singing, talking or listening to him. We can
see the kind of pattern of his praying from what he
taught his disciples, who wanted to enjoy their
prayer times as much as Jesus obviously did.

We deal the Lord's Prayer a great insult if we rattle
it off fast as 'a prayer'. It's far more like a checklist,
or set of headings to remind us that our prayer
needs to spring from

    a) a close relationship with God who loves us and
    b) a loving, accepting relationship with other
        people.

To do today

Take time to pray the Lord's way today. Use the
words in today's reading, but enjoy each section and
think about it, opening up to God your loving parent,
before going on to the next.

PRAYING

Colour the picture as well as you can.

Where is Jesus going to all on his own?
Use the key to crack the code, and write the answer
in the boxes on the next page.

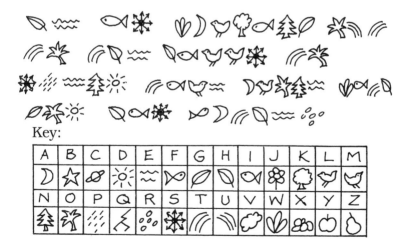

Key:

A	B	C	D	E	F	G	H	I	J	K	L	M
)	☆	∅	☀	≈	🐟	∅	◖	🐟	◁	❀	🌳	🐦

N	O	P	Q	R	S	T	U	V	W	X	Y	Z
🌲	🌴	⫶	⟨	°₀°	❄	⫻	⟍	☁	◊	🍇	🍎	◗

47

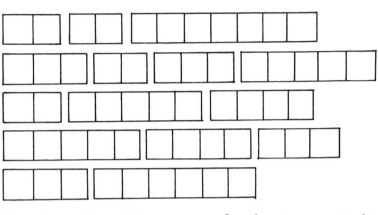

Now try writing this message for the grown ups in code on another piece of paper. (Keep if safe – you'll need it later.)

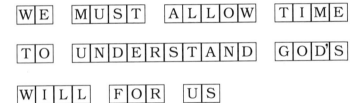

DYING

Read Matthew 27:35-50

One event that is painstakingly recorded in all four gospels is the crucifixion of Jesus. In a sense, all that goes before this – in both Old and New Testaments – leads up to it, and everything after it springs from it. For this is at once the most terrible tragedy and the most hopeful victory of all time. Here is the ultimate length to which love can go: the creative Love which brought all life into existence allows his own life to be bled away at the hands of those who owe him their life. It is an extraordinary event which can show us so much about the nature of Jesus, that millions hang its symbol round their necks or on their walls, to remind them of the incredible extent of God's love for us.

How could it have ever happened that we chose to put God's Son to death? We have been watching all the good that went on in his ministry. We have seen how amazed the crowds were at his signs and healings. So what went wrong?

The first thing we need to be clear about is that no particular group of people was to blame. We can't plead innocence through not being there at the time, because whenever the Christ had come, the same thing would have happened. It was the sin of all time – ours included – which resulted in the nailing up of Jesus to the cross. With his roots in eternity, Jesus felt the weight of all our meanness, our smug complacency, our resentment and our selfishness, together with the abuse of all who have ever and will ever live. And he chose to carry that huge burden through total rejection and death, so as to kill it for us, once and for all.

I suppose we can't appreciate what has been done for us there until we have really tried to pull ourselves up by our own bootstraps – and failed. If you think back over your life, you can probably remember particularly difficult, stressful patches when you were very aware of the limits of your strength and your own resources. Yet those times are often when we have grown and developed most rapidly. It is only when we are simply too exhausted to trust in ourselves any more, that we begin to realise we have been fighting a losing battle all along.

By ourselves we cannot break free of our sin; but the good news is that Jesus is ready and willing to do it in our place – in fact he has already done so. All we need to do is accept that amazing generosity with joy and gratitude. In Jesus, all the sin and spitefulness we loathe in ourselves has been killed off dead. Which means – we are free!

To do today

Imagine yourself standing at the foot of the cross on that hill outside Jerusalem. Don't say anything, just stand there, with Jesus dying above your head. Feel not only his suffering, but also his love for you. Bring to mind the sin and evil in you that you want to be rid of. Know that as he dies, your sin is being killed too. Know that although your sin is painful to him and aiding his death, he is doing this willingly, and he forgives you, because he loves you.

DYING

Read Matthew 27:35-50

Jesus spent about two years as a travelling teacher and healer. During this time he drew great crowds of all ages, and changed many people's lives, setting them free to live life to the full. Yet for the most important part of his ministry in our world we find him left almost alone, rejected and despised. The crowd's taunting voices as he hangs on the cross sound self-righteous and unforgiving. It's like reading those newspapers which enjoy slamming into a former hero. Suddenly everything is wrong about Jesus, and he deserves all he's getting because he hasn't turned out the way they expected. It's a thumbs down verdict.

You've probably been in crowds sometimes, perhaps at a live concert or a football match, where the atmosphere is so highly charged it almost glows! You may have seen films of Hitler, subtly controlling the crowds by using that kind of atmosphere for his own power. It's strange, but a crowd of people is a different animal from all the individual animals who make it up. Jesus once said we were like sheep without a shepherd – or, even worse, perhaps, with false shepherds taking advantage of our herding instinct.

If he had wanted, Jesus could have gone along with the crowd's wishes, and broken free from the cross, called down the wrath of God and struck terror into the hearts of everyone there. He could have saved himself, and for a short time he would have been a hero. The people could have crowned him their king, followed him into battles against the

Romans and ended up with their own country free and probably larger.

But if Jesus had acted in that way, alien to the nature of God, there's no way he could ever again be in a position to buy us back from our slavery in sin. He would no longer have the power of perfect love which is stronger than death. Thankfully, he managed to resist what must been such a strong temptation – to hit back. How it must have hurt as he watched those he loved and longed to set free, totally misunderstanding him. They saw his death on the cross as failure, thinking he'd let them down, when really he was going through this agony because it was the only possible way to save them.

To do today

Cut out any headlines and pictures from this week's newspapers which tell of people hurting and damaging one another. Keep them safe – you'll be using them later.

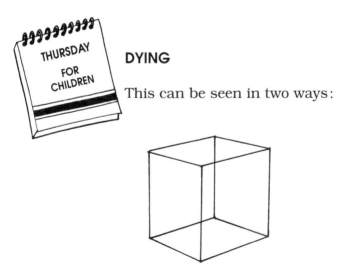

THURSDAY
FOR
CHILDREN

DYING

This can be seen in two ways:

and this:

Can you believe your eyes? Look at this:

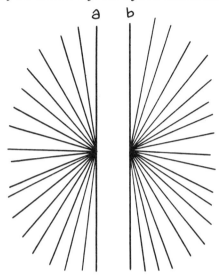

The lines look bent – but check with a ruler

Mark 14:38

Some people hoped that Jesus would lead them in a war against the Romans. They wanted him to be that kind of king.

But Jesus is the King of Love!

Some people thought Jesus was pretending to be God's Son. They thought he deserved to die for that.

But really he WAS God's Son!

Some people saw Jesus was right about loving, but they didn't want to change their lives. They thought they could shut him up by killing him.

But they couldn't – love is stronger than death!

To do today

Colour the picture on page 55 as well as you can, as a way of saying 'Thank you, Jesus, for loving me this much.'

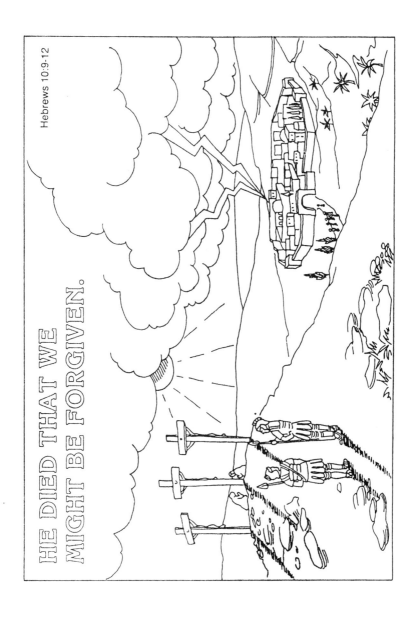

HE DIED THAT WE MIGHT BE FORGIVEN.

Hebrews 10:9-12

RISING TO NEW LIFE

Read one or more of these resurrection accounts: Matthew 28:1-10, Mark 16:1-10, Luke 24:1-12, John 20:1-10

Like the crucifixion, the resurrection is recorded in all four gospels, and referred to frequently in the Acts of the Apostles and in the letters of Paul. It is the glorious completion of the sacrifice offered by Jesus on the previous Friday, and confirms everything that Jesus promised. It would be no good for sin and evil to be killed on that cross, if hope of life had been killed forever at the same time. The cross is only a victory over evil if love emerged beyond death triumphantly alive. And that is exactly what happened.

If you read all four accounts you will begin to see that for every person witnessing the living Jesus after his death and burial, it was a powerfully real and also very personal experience. Already Jesus was able to touch many hearts with hope, encouraging joy and peace, in ways which spoke directly to each individual, even if many were present at the same time. The normal barriers of our kind of life had been broken down and Jesus was free now to be with everyone, everywhere, at any time, giving each one his full attention and love.

Look at the way he appears to people after his resurrection, always starting where their needs are, and reassuring them in the way that will help them most. Take the two disciples who have left Jeru-salem, for instance, and are on their way home to Emmaus. Before Jesus joins them they are miserable and confused, their hopes smashed. What they need is someone to explain how the crucifixion was necessary, and actually a fulfilment of scripture. So Jesus is there to do it. Perhaps they had been thinking, 'If only Jesus was here it would be all right.' In his company it is all right, even though they don't actually recognise him until he breaks bread. But the effect of his appearance is dramatic – they hot-foot it back the 7 miles to Jerusalem in the gathering darkness, full of joy.

Mary Magdalene feels she has lost her dearest friend and Lord. In response, Jesus calls her by name, so that she knows their relationship is just as close as it was. Thomas, who needs physical proof, is provided with it, but finds that looking is quite enough to convince him – Jesus is no longer simply a valuable and highly respected teacher; Thomas now accepts him as his Lord and his God.

And it is the same with us – Jesus meets us in whatever our needs are, and in whatever way is best and most helpful for us. For some, he comes in quiet stillness; for some in ecstatic praise; for some through other people, for some in signs and wonders. We needn't worry about these differences. It is foolish, and a waste of time to do that. The important thing is to recognise and believe that Jesus has passed from death to life, and so is 'available' to be with us wherever we are. Whenever we gather in this firm faith, he will be there among us; and if we live in that faith, we shall find him appearing just as powerfully to us now as he did after the first Easter Day.

To do today

Choose a character whose needs you can recognise in yourself – Mary Magdalene, Thomas, or the Emmaus disciples, for instance – and slowly read over Jesus' appearance to them. Listen to what he says, imagine the setting, the sounds and the smells as if you are there. Then, through the day, keep yourself alert and expectant, ready to recognise Jesus meeting you in love.

RISING TO NEW LIFE

Read Luke 24:1-12

How can anyone come back to life again? That kind of thing just doesn't happen, so how can we be expected to believe it?

If you have questions like this in your mind, sometimes, that's good, because it shows you are thinking seriously, and God wants us to worship him with our minds as well as our hearts. He doesn't want you to go along with believing things just because various adults say so: your questions mean that God is challenging you to work things out for yourself, so that, if you decide to follow Jesus, it will be YOUR decision and no one else's.

So, back to the resurrection and the questions. We often make the mistake of creating for ourselves a nice little matchbox-sized god, who we feel we can control. We can let him out when we feel like it, and slide him out of the way when we want to get on with living our own way. We bring him out at Christmas time, but stick him in the back of a cupboard if he starts showing any real power. The real God is not smaller than we are but infinitely larger.

When you think of the size of our Milky Way galaxy, and realise that's only one galaxy out of millions, it makes you feel pretty small! Well, God is the power and energy and love which brought all that into being. He can be dangerous, and we're only alive now because he wants it that way. It's hardly surprising that our minds, small as they are, can't understand the great, powerful mind of God. What is totally impossible for us is certainly not impossible for him. In fact, when you think of that galactic-sized power of positive love and goodness, the resurrection becomes a very natural event, perfectly in keeping with what we know of God.

And that's where the crunch is – if Jesus was just human, then the resurrection couldn't have happened; but if Jesus was also God, then the resurrection is the only thing that COULD happen. That startling truth about Jesus – that he is God as well as man – exploded in people's hearts and minds as they experienced him alive among them.

To do today

Read through Luke 24:33-43 and imagine you are there with the disciples. In your mind's eye, see where everyone is standing/sitting, notice what they're wearing and what they're talking about. Now you are suddenly aware of Jesus, standing among you. What goes through your mind? How does everyone react? What is Jesus doing and saying? As you imagine it, let Jesus reach you and touch you.

RISING TO NEW LIFE

What happened when Jesus had died on the cross on Good Friday?

His friends buried him in a tomb and sealed it up with a huge, heavy stone.

Write the answer here:

_ _ _   _ _ _ _ _ _ _   _ _ _ _ _ _

_ _ _   _ _   _   _ _ _ _   _ _ _

_ _ _ _ _   _ _   _ _   _ _ _ _

_   _ _ _ _   _ _ _ _ _   _ _ _ _ _ _.

What happened on Sunday morning?

To do today

Colour in the dotty bits

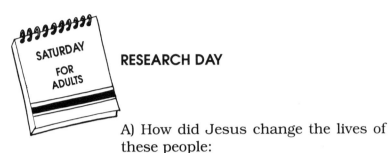

RESEARCH DAY

A) How did Jesus change the lives of these people:

Bartimaeus	Jairus	The young rich man	Levi

Mark 10:46-52	Mark 5:21-42	Matthew 19:16-30	Mark 2:13-17

B) Read Exodus 31:12-17, followed by Luke 6:6-11. How were the Pharisees right about Jesus and how were they mistaken?

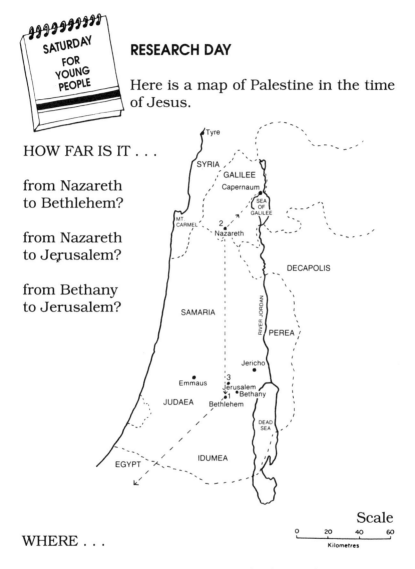

SATURDAY FOR YOUNG PEOPLE

RESEARCH DAY

Here is a map of Palestine in the time of Jesus.

HOW FAR IS IT . . .

from Nazareth
to Bethlehem?

from Nazareth
to Jerusalem?

from Bethany
to Jerusalem?

Scale

0   20   40   60

Kilometres

WHERE . . .

did Jesus turn water into wine? (John 2:1)
was the Roman centurion's servant cured?
(Matthew 8:5-13)
was the blind man given sight? (Luke 18:35-43)

63

ACTIVITY DAY

Today you are going to make:

A CROSS OF PAIN AND LOVE

You will need:

Two rough pieces of wood
Nails or some string
Some thin garden wire
Some fresh flowers and oasis
A pot of earth

What you do:

1. Join the two pieces of wood to make a cross. (You may need someone to help you with this.)

2. 'Plant' the cross in a pot of earth.

3. Bend and twist the wire all around the cross to look like the pain and hurt of Jesus. Hammer in some nails, if you like. (Mind your fingers!)

4. Soak the oasis and wedge it in amongst the wire.

5. Now push fresh flowers into the oasis to look like the love and kindness of Jesus.

Bring your cross of pain and love to the 'Together in Christ' session to teach the others.

TOGETHER IN CHRIST 2

Part 1
While everyone gathers, try decoding the children's messages.
Hold hands in a circle with the children's crosses in the centre and remember what Jesus promised – 'When two or three are gathered together in my name, there I am among them'. Sing together: *Father, we adore you* (OANA 114).

Let the children come into the centre and hold their crosses. Adults and young people are going to find out what the crosses mean. What does the wire show? What do the flowers show? The children can explain.

Part 2
Split into small, mixed groups of 3-6 people. Work on making a living picture (a tableau) of one event in Jesus' life (such as his birth, his ministry, his death, his appearance after the resurrection). You have 5 minutes! When everyone is ready, look at each group's tableau in turn, in the right time sequence. If there is only one group, try making another tableau together. As you watch one another, sing: *Jesus, name above all names* (OANA 265), so that this becomes an act of loving worship.

Part 3
Stay in the same groups to discuss this week's questions.
1. Where was Jesus living and working when he lived on earth? (The young people have maps and distances to help you.)
2. What kind of things was he doing in his ministry?

3. Why did Jesus have to suffer and be killed? (Look at the newspaper pictures.)
4. How did his crucifixion help you and me?
5. What happened on the Sunday after Good Friday?
6. What does the resurrection tell us about Jesus?

Part 4
Come together to praise God, and thank him for his great love. Sing a hymn or chorus such as:

> *You give me peace* (Ishmael Praise Party Vol. 3)
> *Give thanks with a grateful heart* (SOF4 27)
> *I rejoice* (Ishmael Praise Party Vol. 2)
> *My song is love unknown* (OANA 337)

and finish with a shared hug of peace.

WEEK THREE
WHAT IS HE SAYING?

I AM THE GOOD SHEPHERD
Read John 10:7-16

Last week we were wandering around Palestine, watching Jesus as he worked among those he loved and had been sent to help. As we saw what he was doing, we got to know him better. This week we shall be mingling with the crowds, listening to what Jesus is saying, hearing his teaching, his encouragement, and his warnings.

People jostled to hear him – nobody had to persuade them to come, they just arrived; hanging on to his words, enjoying his stories, impressed by his authority, challenged, shocked, comforted and helped as they sat on the grass or beside the water in the sun and wind. That's where we will join them, because through the Holy Spirit his words echo down through time, and will reach us with as much impact and power as they had at the beginning.

We start with these wonderfully reassuring words – 'I am the good shepherd'. Jesus often talked about sheep since there were a lot of them around at the time, and, as we know, he always starts where people are! When one sheep decides to move, the whole lot move; sheep can plan as far as the next mouthful, but often get themselves into danger through looking only at their immediate needs; sheep are prey to attacking animals, and they panic easily, scattering in all directions. Don't these characteristics sound familiar?

When Jesus tells us he is the good shepherd, he is

speaking to the deep anxiety and apprehension we have about the state of our world, and where we are heading. He is assuring us of peace of mind, shelter, and the kind of care that allows us to relax, without worrying so much about everything. He can take all that weight off our shoulders and enable us to be carefree and lighthearted, enjoying the present moment and knowing that our shepherd will look after us, guarding us with his life. The promise is not on offer for a limited time only, either. It's not like us enjoying being waited on during a few days' holiday but knowing we've got to return to the grind for the rest of the year.

Living with Jesus as our good shepherd is rather like being on holiday all the time – if we know ourselves to be in his good care, strain disappears and we are free. In that state, whatever difficulties we face we shall find an inner peace, which anchors us and gives us a security that nothing and no one else can provide.

To do today

Deliberately and regularly throughout the day, cast your cares on Jesus – allow him to be your good shepherd and enjoy the freedom of being one of his lambs.

I AM THE GOOD SHEPHERD
Read John 10:7-16

Have you ever done something you know was pretty stupid, but you did it anyway because everyone else was? Or perhaps at some time you've had an argument with your parents over them wanting you to wear/do something which your friends would think ridiculous?

It's important to us to feel part of a group, and we are quite like sheep in the way we tend to conform to the behaviour of others in our particular 'flock'. Mind you, if we just go wherever the other sheep go, we're quite likely to get ourselves into difficulties.

Jesus obviously liked sheep. As a child, he probably helped look after the local sheep on the hills, along with all the other village children – sheep-minding was the equivalent of our paper rounds! Perhaps it was then that he noticed the difference between shepherds who owned their sheep, and shepherds who were just hired. As you might expect, those whose sheep belonged to them took a great deal more care about them, and made certain the animals were safe, well-fed and watered, and in no danger from predators. The hired shepherds had nothing to gain by putting themselves in danger for the sheep's sake, so they would do the bare minimum, and if danger threatened, they were off.

That's why Jesus talked of himself as being our 'good shepherd'. He understands the way we all herd together, and don't always notice that we're edging towards the sheer drop of a steep cliff. He knows what it feels like to be human because he was human, too. But, being God as well, he can be the best shepherd any sheep could ever bleat for! He never puts us on leads, never trains us for circus acts – he lets us get on with being ourselves, while providing all the loving care and protection we need. When the grass gets thin in one area of our lives, he will lead us on to rich meadows he knows about, but we don't. So, if we are going through a difficult patch in life, we can be certain that our good shepherd will find the best track for us – and even carry us if necessary – towards safer ground.

To do today

Find a quiet time at some point today – the bath-room, as a last resort! – and think about your life at the moment, especially any sticky or uncomfortable parts of it. If they're there, don't pretend they're not. Don't fool yourself that you can handle them on your own. Go to Jesus as your good shepherd and put yourself under his leadership as simply as if you were a sheep; just trust him with what you've told him. Trust him to lead you safely through.

I AM THE GOOD SHEPHERD

Can you help this shepherd count all his sheep?

Have you got a pet? If you have, draw it here. If you haven't, draw the kind of pet you would like to have.

My pet's name is _____

Now fill in this chart

LOOKING AFTER YOUR PET	Twice a day or more	Once a day	Once a week	Some-times
We give our pet some food				
We give our pet some drink				
We play with our pet				
We clean our pet's home				
We check our pet is safe				
We take our pet to the vet				

Jesus said he is our shepherd. That makes us his

Jesus looks after us. He gives us food and drink. He keeps us safe. He shows us the right way to go when we are muddled. He helps us to be helpful and kind. He comforts us when we are sad or in pain.

To do today

Help the shepherd search for his lost sheep.

If you get sad today, little lamb, tell your good shepherd about it. The way he helps you may not be the way you expect. You may just suddenly feel happier. You may find that you're still sad, but it doesn't hurt so much. You may be given someone or something to cheer you up. You may find your sadness lets you help someone else in some way.

Whatever way Jesus helps, it will be the best way, not just for you, but for his other lambs, too!

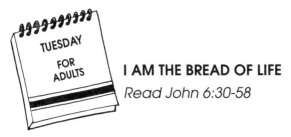

I AM THE BREAD OF LIFE
Read John 6:30-58

When at the start of his ministry Jesus had been tempted in the desert to turn stones into bread, he had resisted temptation with these words from scripture: 'Man cannot live by bread alone, but by every word that proceeds from the mouth of God.' For Jesus, his Father's words, his Father's will for him, were as nourishing as real food. And when Jesus feeds the 5000 people, he uses that feeding to explain how he, the Word of God, can nourish them more fully and permanently than any wheat bread. He expresses this truth powerfully, with a forceful parable. He describes feeding on the Word of God as actually eating his flesh and drinking his blood – a scandalous and violently thought-provoking parable, to which many, not surprisingly, took exception.

No wonder that later, after many followers have left in disgust, Jesus is so delighted that Peter says, 'Lord, to whom would we go? You have *the words that give eternal life.*' Peter's words show that he understands exactly what Jesus has been saying. He understands that Jesus himself is God's nourishing Word, and we need to 'feed' on him and depend on him for spiritual, eternal life, rather than living a purely physical life dependent on bread. Peter must have been listening and understanding with God-given insight and wisdom. He is thinking with the mind of God.

For us, the problem is not the shock of hearing the truth in such a powerful, unusual way, but the blindness of familiarity that comes from hearing the words so often. If we are not careful, the words we know so well just trickle over the surface of our minds and don't impinge at all. So if for a moment we listen to Jesus speaking here, some time *before* the Last Supper and the crucifixion, we shall feel the impact more directly. 'You need bread to eat so as to stay alive,' Jesus is saying, 'But with bread you will always get hungry again. If you feed on the Word of God – if you eat me – you will find you are satisfied, and this bread will keep you alive through eternity, not just through your lifetime.'

Suddenly we are challenged to eat God's Word as we would eat bread – not just glancing over it once a day, or hearing it once a week in church. If we just glanced at a loaf it wouldn't fill us up much! Instead we are to bite into it, chew on it, take it right into ourselves and allow it to be digested, so that it does us good, gives us energy and actually goes towards building and repairing us spiritually. And as if that wasn't enough, Jesus tells us that he himself is the Word of God personified. Everything he is, and does, and says, both now and in the Bible, is a personification of God's Word – Jesus is God expressing himself in our language.

To do today

Take a small bite of this bread (John 6:33) and chew on it well, swallow it and allow it to nourish your whole self.

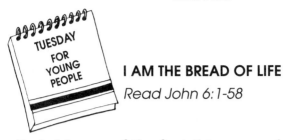

I AM THE BREAD OF LIFE

Read John 6:1-58

Probably one of the first things you do when you get in from school or work is to raid the fridge or the biscuit tin. Eating is a top priority, especially while you're still growing. I can remember demolishing half a loaf with butter and marmalade on it (I did cut it in slices!) before I could think about doing anything else. One of my children always heads for cold potatoes. There's no accounting for taste! We go on stuffing our mouths until we get that comfortable feeling inside which tells us our bodies are satisfied, and have the fuel they need for the moment. An hour or two later, they'll be nagging us to eat again. It's a good thing they do – if we never knew we were hungry, we might not bother to eat, and then we would, quite simply, die. It's as basic an essential as that – eating is a matter of life and death.

Jesus knew all about our need for bread. He shared the need, because he was human, and we all need to eat, whatever our bodies look like and however old we are. So when Jesus wanted to explain an important truth in a way that everyone could understand, he chose an experience that every one of us has regularly – eating! He fed 5000 people with enough to satisfy them completely, and then, when they got hungry again, explained to them that we need spiritual feeding with God's word, just as much as we need physical feeding.

It isn't a lot of help if someone tells you what you need, but doesn't tell you where you can get hold of it. If your friends know exactly what kind of jeans or suncream you need, they will probably suggest a shop that stocks that brand. The chances are that your friends know because they've been there themselves.

Well, when Jesus says to us that we need 'food' to feed us spiritually, he also tells us where to get it. 'Come to me,' he says, 'because I am the bread you need. I am the bread of God's Word, and if you eat this bread – me – you will feel completely satisfied; and you will keep alive and well, even when your body wears out.'

To do today

Take a bite of God's word (John 6:37) and eat it, enjoying the taste, chewing on it and swallowing it so that it can nourish you.

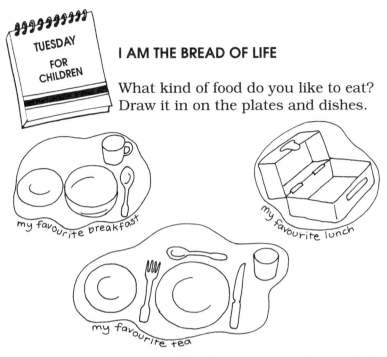

I AM THE BREAD OF LIFE

What kind of food do you like to eat? Draw it in on the plates and dishes.

Does your tummy rumble when you are hungry? So does mine. That's how we know our bodies need more food. When we eat, our bodies are happy. They can grow and run and fight off diseases. If we don't eat at all, our bodies die.

YOU need food as well as your body. Hugs are a kind of food that makes us feel well-fed with love. So are smiles and friendly words. When you give those things to your family and friends, you are feeding them! And when you are given hugs and kind words, YOU are being fed.

To do today

Be generous with your hugs and smiles and friendly words today – someone you love may be feeling 'hungry'!

THE KINGDOM OF GOD IS LIKE . . .
Read Matthew 13:24-33; 44-46

If Jesus had given the crowds long, learned sermons way above their heads, I do not think the crowds would have lasted long! Some might have tried to understand, but most would drift back to getting on with ordinary living as best they could, convinced that his message was not really meant for them. But Jesus really loved them, and true love would never allow him to leave them feeling such detachment or rejection. So he spoke to them often in parables – stories which were funny, ludicrous, shocking, touching or puzzling. They contained secret truths if you were listening with your heart as well as your ears, and they were very entertaining however you listened.

Many of these stories described the inner workings of God and the kingdom of heaven. It's as if Jesus, being on the 'inside', so to speak, is inviting us behind the scenes of the ten commandments to see God's preposterously generous love in working clothes.

Finding the kingdom of heaven, says Jesus, is like a man finding treasure in a field which he's so excited about that he is prepared to sell all his possessions in order to get hold of. It's like the delight you feel when you find something very precious to you which you had lost. God is like a delighted father welcoming a son who had left him and lived recklessly and selfishly, and now comes home at last. He is like a compassionate employer who lets his employees off massive debts, but expects similar generosity to filter through the whole company. God is like a shepherd taking as much trouble over one sheep who has got himself in a tight spot, as over all the other sheep.

The kingdom starts little, Jesus explains, like a mustard seed, or a scrap of yeast, but it grows far bigger than you'd expect from looking at its beginnings. It can't grow effectively unless it's in receptive soil, with no choking weeds around. It may need pruning, too.

In this kingdom, love and care extend to those who intimidate you or put you down, as well as your friends. In this kingdom, there is abandoned giving and forgiving which is crazy by any worldly kingdom's standards.

All the time Jesus uses local characters and familiar scenarios to give the people an increasingly clear idea of whom they worship and how they can live the way of love. We all know about losing and finding things, growing food, honouring debts, lending, borrowing and so on; and we can all laugh at cartoon pictures of someone with a plank in his eye trying to get a speck of dust out of his friend's eye, or one blind man trying to lead another, and them both ending up in the ditch.

So, as we start listening to Jesus' stories, both in the Bible and in the ordinary events of our lives, we can begin to understand more and more the character of our God, and the nature of the kingdom we belong to.

To do today

Ask Jesus to teach you more about God's love, and walk through the day with your spiritual eyes and ears open to notice what he is saying through ordinary circumstances.

THE KINGDOM OF GOD IS LIKE . . .
Read Matthew 13:24-33

Tom and Sally lived in a large detached house in Surrey. Tom had built up his own business and owned a textiles factory. They had two sons, Pete and Mike. When the younger son, Mike, turned 18, he asked his Dad to let him cash his massive insurance policy and he went to live in a smart part of London. He spent a lot of time in various nightclubs, ate in all the best restaurants, took up speedo racing and paragliding, and had plenty of girl friends, one of whom had won a Miss World title. He had a great time, and only ever wore handmade silk shirts.

The trouble was, his money ran out, and he got evicted from his penthouse. He took a room at a squalid bedsit apartment block along with three others who were all into drugs. To drown his feelings of failure, he started a drug habit himself, and soon lost his job as a hotel cleaner. Gradually his life degenerated into a blur of highs and times of abject misery, filth and guilt. He had long since broken off all correspondence with his family, shying away from the lies about the fabulous time he was having and how popular he was.

One day he was waking up after sleeping rough in a park when a small child came running past, singing to herself, going to feed the ducks with bread. When the child caught sight of Mike, she screamed and ran to her Dad, crying. Suddenly Mike realised how much he loathed himself and what he had become. For the first time he admitted to himself that he had a problem, and that he needed help. He even began to think that, with a spell on one of those rehabilitation courses, there might be some hope. More than anything he longed to see his Dad again.

Then he glanced down at his body. He knew he could never go home – his father wouldn't even recognise him like this, and he'd have every right to chuck him out, disgusted. Then he had another idea. He remembered the men who worked on the shop floor in the textiles factory. Even if he couldn't be his father's son any more, perhaps his Dad would give him a job in the factory. Mike walked down through the city, and along beside the A20, with cars screaming past him and the rain streaming down.

When he got to the bottom of his parents' drive-way, his Dad was staring out of the study window, and suddenly their eyes met. Mike's Dad wasn't as fit as he had been, but he ran out of the house with the old black labrador at his heels, and down the drive to his son. Mike could hardly bear to see the joy on his Dad's face; it made him realise how badly he had let him down. 'I thought perhaps you might give me a cleaning job in the factory . . . 'Mike started to mumble. But his Dad just hugged him, the tears pouring down his face. 'I thought you were dead, Mike!' he kept saying, 'but you're alive! My son Mike's still alive!' And together they walked back up to the house, with the dog barking excitedly around them.

And that, says Jesus, is how God our Father is with us: that loving; that welcoming; that forgiving.

To do today

Try thinking out a modern version of another of Jesus' parables, so as to bring out the meaning. Here are some stories to choose from:

The lost sheep (Matthew 18:10-14).
The lost coin (Luke 15:8-10).
The good Samaritan (Luke 10:29-37).
The rich fool (Luke 12:16-21).

THE KINGDOM OF GOD IS LIKE . . .

Jesus told lots of good stories. Here is one of them. Can you read it?

' 1 day a 🐑 wandered off on his own. He came to a steep ⛰ and saw some juicy 🌿 growing on a ledge below. He jumped ⬇ and ate the 🌿 . But he couldn't get ⬆ the steep ⛰ again! The 🐑 tried to get 🐑 a different way, but the more he tried the more lost he became. It was getting 🌥 now with the ⭐ and the 🌙 in the sky. Meanwhile, the 🧑 was putting all the 🐑🐑 in their 📦 for the night, and he counted each 1 . He knew there should be 100 , but he noticed there were only 99 🐑 . 1 🐑 was missing! So the 🧑 left the other 🐑 safely in their 📦 and set out over the 🏔 2 find his lost 🐑 . At last he heard a faint 🗨baa! baa! and 🧑 towards the sound.

83

There was the ⟨sheep⟩ , feeling lost and scared. The ⟨shepherd⟩ lifted the sheep on to his ⟨shoulders⟩ and carried him over the ⟨hills⟩ under the ⟨stars⟩ and ⟨moon⟩ until they reached home. The ⟨sheep⟩ was very ☺ to have ⟨sheep⟩ found. The ⟨shepherd⟩ was very ☺ to have found his lost ⟨sheep⟩.'

Jesus said that God our Father is like that shepherd. He loves each one of us, and each of us is important and special to him. It makes him really happy whenever a person who has led a bad, selfish or unkind life, is brought back home again.

WHAT IS GOD'S KINGDOM LIKE?
(READ LUKE 13:18-19)

A ⟨man⟩ takes a ∘ _ _ _ _ _ _ _ _ and plants it in his _ _ _ _ _ _.

_ _ _

The plant _ _ _ _ _ and becomes a _ _ _ _ _,

and the ⟨birds⟩ make their _ _ _ _ _ _ _ _

in its _ _ _ _ _ _ _

To do today

Make this model of Jesus telling a story to the crowds to teach them more about God, his Father.

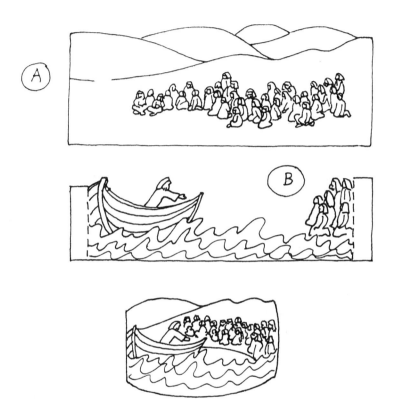

Copy a) and b) and cut them out carefully. Stick the flaps on b) round the back of a) at the sides, so that a) is bent into a curve. Now your model will stand up.

LOVE ONE ANOTHER
Read John 13:34-35

All through his ministry Jesus had been telling stories to explain the practical, generous nature of God's love. Now, not long before the crucifixion, we find him giving a direct command to his disciples: 'Love one another.' The fact that it is definitely a command tells us a lot about the kind of love Jesus meant. You can't, for instance, command someone to love in the sense of falling in love. Nor can it be the kind of love which floods out when we feel emotionally charged and dribbles out when we're tired and having an off-day.

Jesus is commanding us to love one another in the same way that he has loved us. His love is, as we have already discovered, the expression of our heavenly Father's love, and that love is what Jesus has been describing in all those parables. It is thoroughly practical; it is directed at the unworthy just as much as the worthy; it is both spontaneous and habitual; it involves passionate sorrow and outrage against evil, coupled with abandoned delight at reconciliation and all goodness. It is filled with hope, and it goes on and on regardless of circumstances.

Writing this, working only from the parables, I have just realised how familiar it sounds – Paul has described it far more beautifully in his letter to the Christians in Corinth. (1 Corinthians 13:1-13). Millions of Christians through the ages have shown it beautifully in their lives, and it is always relevant to every generation in every culture.

No wonder Jesus says everyone will know we are

his disciples if we love in this way. We will stick out a mile! As Jesus said, everyone can love those who love them. It takes quite a different quality to act with really caring love even towards those who hate us and treat us badly. To do so we must be prepared to become fools for Christ's sake, and give up all ambitions for lining our own nests and establishing a quiet, comfortable life-style. Loving, Jesus-shaped, is bound to lead us into all kinds of difficulties and even dangers, because it means allowing ourselves to be vulnerable, just as Jesus did when he was born into our world as a human baby.

To do today

Find 1 Corinthians 13:1-13 and read through it slowly and thoughtfully. Then read it again, inserting your own name in place of the world 'Love' all through it. That is an eye opener, both to our failures and to our true calling.

THURSDAY FOR YOUNG PEOPLE

LOVE ONE ANOTHER
Read John 13:34-35

We hear an awful lot about love. Just think of all the music which is about getting together or breaking up. Think of all those magazine stories where, in spite of terrible problems along the way the couple who are meant for each other finally get together. Then there are all the adverts which are designed to appeal to our hopes of wonderful, romantic relationships with Someone exactly right for us.

That's all the glossy paper image of love, of course. In real life we may find ourselves on the receiving end of spiteful words in an argument before a break up with someone; or shuffled between split parents who no longer love one another, though we may still love both of them. Love, when it goes wrong, can be miserable and painful for everyone involved. Perhaps, if you have already been badly hurt, you are rather disillusioned with the idea of love. Perhaps, if your romantic life is going really well for you at the moment, you think it's the best thing ever.

But if love is such a volatile, unpredictable thing, why did Jesus go and command us to do it? Wasn't that rather foolhardy of him? The answer lies in the kind of love he meant. He was talking about the love that father had in the story yesterday – the one who was so ready to forgive and welcomed his son back so happily. It's the kind of love you saw in the parable you chose to tell in a modern version. Perhaps you can think of some relationships where that sort of love is so badly needed, and people's lives struggle on in misery without it. We only have to look at the news each day to see situations crying out for it and disasters happening because it isn't anywhere to be seen.

Jesus can command us to do it because his love isn't tied to our emotions or sexual instincts, so we don't necessarily have to feel like loving in order to do it. We can decide to act with practical, caring love, whether it's towards a really attractive person or one who irritates us immensely and doesn't understand us at all. And that's the kind of love which will make us stand out as being followers of Jesus, because it is totally crazy love, by most people's standards. By God's standards, it's the only love worth giving.

To do today

Practise this kind of loving towards those you would normally ignore, and those who irritate you. Do it for Jesus, not for yourself, and you will find you won't be put off when you're rejected or laughed at for what you are doing. You may even find you enjoy it!

LOVE ONE ANOTHER

When Jesus tells us to love one another, he wants us to be kind and thoughtful, friendly and helpful to *everyone*, even the ones we don't like much, and those who are not always kind to us. That's hard! But Jesus has promised to help us.

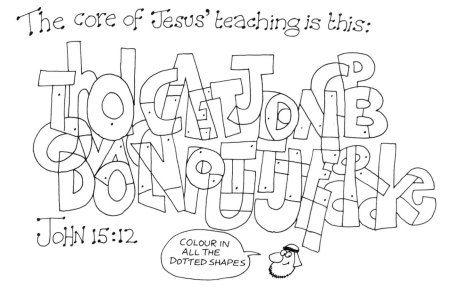

The core of Jesus' teaching is this:

JOHN 15:12

COLOUR IN ALL THE DOTTED SHAPES

89

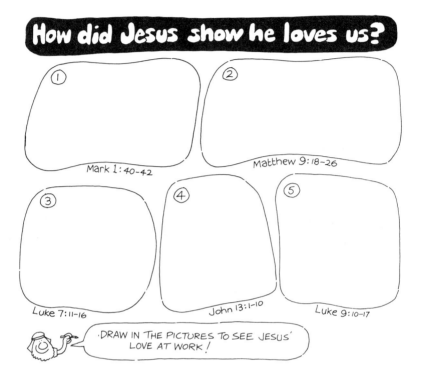

To do today

Do something kind for someone you are not usually kind to.

DO THIS . . .
Read Luke 22:19-20

The ten commandments of the Old Covenant had been full of 'Thou shalt not's' – commands about what we mustn't do in order to stay within the pact God had made with his people. Jesus, the direct expression of God the Father, chooses to express God's Way, or Law, in positive terms – 'Love God and love your neighbour as yourself.' And in the same way, at the Last Supper, the command Jesus gives us is a positive, active one: 'Do this in memory of me.'

When we hear the words so often, at every Eucharist, we can all too easily drift into taking them for granted, and lose the startling impact of what is actually going on here. So let's creep in to that upper room with the disciples, adjust our eyes to the dim candle light, and see there whatever our Lord wants to show us.

Remember that Jesus knew at this point that he could not avoid being put to death, and he had a pretty clear idea of what a tortured death it would be. He also knew his friends very well; he loved them and understood their human needs. From his constant communion with his Father, he knew the importance of being spiritually as well as physically fed on a regular basis.

With God's amazing sense of timing, this meal was being celebrated as the feast of Passover, when God's covenant with his people was remembered, and the sacrificed lamb's blood had been sprinkled as a sign on the door posts so the angel of death passed over their homes. Passover celebrated the fact that God loved his people, and had set them free from slavery.

Now, here is Jesus giving the Passover a new and remarkable meaning. Through his impending sacrifice all people are set free – not from external bondage, but from the real fetters of self-centredness and sin. As we eat the bread at every Communion, we are taking in the spiritual nourishment of Jesus himself; taking on board the capacity for the kind of loving that gives everything, even life.

Jesus is giving us a tangible sign of his presence with us through all the years before his glorious return, whenever that may be. When we all go our various ways after sharing Communion, we are carriers of Christ by virtue of his body being 'broken', or expended in total love. As his carriers, we are empowered and called to love to the same extent.

To do today

Pray that when you next receive Communion, you will be reminded of both the privilege and the responsibility of what you are doing.

DO THIS . . .
Read Luke 22:19-20

You've probably brought home the odd (sometimes very odd!) souvenir from different holidays. Often things like this get stuck away under a heap in a cupboard, and you come across them by accident when you're hunting for something else. They're just the sort of things to side-track you, and leave you staring into space, re-living the memories they bring back, instead of getting on with whatever it was you were meant to be doing.

The cartoon image of an American tourist is a camera-clicking guy, who spends so much time peering down the viewfinder that he's in danger of missing the live performance! I'm sure this happens because the tours are often so crammed with sight-seeing that the tourists feel desperate to capture as much as possible on film. That way their memories will be jogged later on to remember more than just a kaleidoscopic blur.

Most of us have fairly short memories and need help in remembering things. I suppose that's why diaries are so popular. Jesus knew that his followers would need something to remind them of his contin-uing love, and the importance of his saving death. What better sign to choose than a shared meal, using bread – such a widespread and simple food.

The fact that it was bread would remind his fol-lowers that he was feeding them (not only physically, but spiritually as well). The fact that it was Passover would show his followers that Jesus was setting them free from slavery – slavery to self and sin, that is. And the fact that he told them the bread was his body meant that, in sharing the bread, his followers would be able to share Jesus' life, including his will-ingness to give his whole life serving others in love.

Jesus doesn't just advise us to 'Do this'; he doesn't just give it a five-star recommendation. He tells us to do it. And every time we do, whether very simply with just a few people there, or at a huge open-air fellowship, Jesus comes and gives us himself. You are only you, and I am only me, but Jesus is ready and willing to come and live in us.

To do today

Start giving thanks to God for your food before you eat it. You don't have to say it aloud – you don't need to use any set form. But if you get into the habit of saying a blessing each time you eat, then your food will become a way of reminding you to keep in touch with Jesus.

DO THIS . . .

On the next page there is a picture of the last supper Jesus ate with his friends before he died. Can you see what they had to eat and drink?

Jesus knew he was going to die on the cross, and he wanted his friends to know he would still be with them. The bread and wine are his sign to us that he is still with us. Jesus feeds us with his life, so we can love as he loves us. When have you seen bread and wine in church?

Break the code to find out what Jesus said

1	2	3	4	5	6	7	8	9	10
B	D	H	I	L	M	O	S	T	Y

```
_  _  _  _    _  _    _  _
9  3  4  8    4  8    6  10

_  _  _  _    _  _  _  _
1  7  2  10   9  3  4  8

_  _  _  _    _  _  _  _  _
4  8  6  10   1  5  7  7  2
```

To do today

Colour the picture on page 95 as carefully as you can.

RESEARCH DAY

Much of Jesus' teaching, and many of his sayings, are collected together in Matthew, chapters 5, 6 and 7. It is worth taking the time to read these three chapters straight off at one sitting for a change, because they will give you a good, overall view of what Jesus was saying when he taught the crowds. As you read, try as far as possible to forget that you have heard the words before. Imagine yourself sitting squashed up between two or three other people on the grass as you listen to Jesus speaking. Then he will be able to speak directly to your own particular needs or problems.

RESEARCH DAY

Spend today's session having a look at two other parables of Jesus – the man who builds a tower, and the king with his army. You'll find them in Luke 14:25-33. Think about them. What do you reckon they mean? How can we give up 'everything'? Can you think of anyone you know who has?

ACTIVITY DAY

Clever cutting! First of all, write the word LOVE in big letters on a plain sheet of paper. At the moment you couldn't fit anyone inside that little thing, could you? Well, if you cut the paper exactly as I have shown you here,

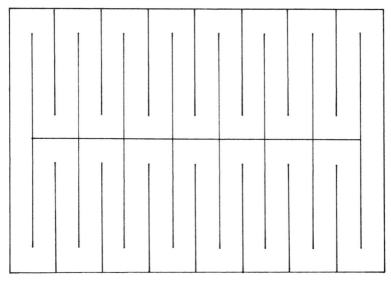

(Folding the paper in half makes it easier to cut.)

you will find that it will fit round quite a lot of people! Try it and see; you may need one or two goes before you get it right.

Get another sheet of paper ready (with LOVE already written on it) and bring it with you to this week's 'Together in Christ' session. Bring along a pair of scissors as well, so you can cut it there and give everyone a surprise!

TOGETHER IN CHRIST 3

Part 1
Begin with a short time of stillness, asking Jesus to be among you and lead your thinking.

The children show their sheets of paper with LOVE written on them. Everyone can watch as the children cut the paper up. God's love, too, is much bigger than we sometimes realise! See how many people will fit in the love chains. Make sure there are mixed ages in each group, and see how the 'love' surrounding you makes you get 'closer' to those around you. While still in the love chains, sing: *Jesus, Jesus, can I tell you what I know* (MSOTS 145).

Part 2
Split into all-age groups of 3-6 people to discuss the following questions:
1. What are some of the things Jesus said during his ministry on earth? Go round the group so that everyone can say what they particularly noticed. Never mind if several people choose the same things – that may point to those things being very important for the group.

2. How is Jesus our good shepherd?

3. In what ways has Jesus 'fed' you during this week?

4. Where is God's kind of love particularly needed in our world at the moment?

5. What did Jesus do with the bread and wine at the Last Supper?

6. If you receive Communion, what does it mean to you, and why do you do it?

Part 3

Sit round in a circle, and listen to the young people telling their modern versions of some of the parables. If you wish, someone could read the version of the lost son on page 81 of this book.

Part 4

Sing together a chorus or hymn to praise God for the way he speaks through his Son. Here are some suggestions:

> *Love is something if you give it away* (Alleluia! 10)
> *Peace, perfect peace is the gift* (OANA 411)
> *A new commandment* (OANA 29)
> *Make me a channel of your peace* (OANA 320)

Finish with a shared hug of peace, making sure no one is left out by anyone!

WEEK FOUR
WHO DOES HE MIX WITH?

MARY

Read John 2:1-12

When I was a child, my mother used to say, 'When you find someone you want to marry, make sure you look at his parents before you decide!' Now there's a wise woman for you.

We are going to continue our search for Jesus by looking at who he mixes with, and we need to start with his mother, Mary, who carried him through pregnancy, gave birth to him, nursed and nurtured him to manhood. What was she like, and what kind of relationship did she and her Son have?

Luke gives us many glimpses of Mary. We see her willing response to Gabriel, God's messenger: 'I am the Lord's servant; may it happen to me as you have said.' She couldn't possibly have reacted so positively and calmly unless she was already very close to her Lord. We sense that calm flexibility in the whole story of Jesus' birth with all its potential traumas. And we know that Mary was the kind of person to think things over quietly in her heart, rather than dashing about telling everyone. During his childhood, Jesus was protected by her quiet nature, and allowed a normal, natural upbringing. Mary was not the sort to sell her story to the press!

We know that, like any parent, she had her times of worry and there must have been many occasions, apart from the recorded visit to the temple, when she found it hard to understand her child. By the time we see them together at the wedding at Cana, it is clear that they must have often talked over who Jesus was and what his mission would be. Mary obviously has complete faith in him to put things right. Perhaps she already had experience of this in the privacy of their home? At any rate, she just comes quietly to Jesus and tells him the problem. Jesus' reply shows they must have often discussed when his time would come, and Jesus still has a hesitancy which Mary, as his parent, obviously recognises. She senses that this is one of those occasions when Jesus needs reassurance that the time is right, and she acts accordingly. We need to remember that this was, according to John, the first sign Jesus performed.

Mary was still with her Son at the foot of the cross, and she was among the first to see him after the resurrection. Quite a mother. We have so much to thank her for.

To do today

Read through the first two chapters of Luke, concentrating on Mary – get to know her through what she says and doesn't say; what she does and doesn't do.

MARY

Read John 2:1-12

There's no one quite like your Mum, is there! OK, so you have your differences from time to time, and you get on one another's nerves quite often, but you love her, and you know she loves you and will still fuss over you even now if you give her half a chance.

Maybe every birthday you hear all the gory details about the day she had you, or, if you're adopted, the day she chose you and brought you home. Or perhaps you don't get to see your Mum too often, and miss her. Mums are certainly special, and we've all got one – we all had someone who lugged us around inside them for about nine months and then worked very hard for a day or so to get us out into this world. And we all take after our parents in our looks and characteristics to some extent.

Jesus, too, had a mother who had brought him into the world, and he probably looked like her. The way Mary and Joseph brought Jesus up must have affected the way he turned out, just as our upbringing is bound to affect our development. We know that Joseph was a carpenter, and that he didn't get flustered easily, even though he had plenty he could have panicked about. He was strong, capable and kind, and it's thought he must have already died by the time his Son was in his early thirties.

What about Mary? We know that she didn't hesitate to accept God's will for her, though she must have guessed that life could never be the same after this, and would not always be a bed of roses. We know she was thoughtful and calm, loyal and always ready to change her lifestyle if necessary. She and Jesus were obviously very fond of one another, and must have often talked about his ministry and what the events at his birth meant.

Now, at the wedding, she has no doubt that Jesus can put things right. Jesus may not have been accepted by the people in his home town of Nazareth, but he was certainly believed in by his Mum! Although Jesus is hesitant about showing his power at this early stage, Mary understands that the time is right. As his mother, she knew the difference between her Son giving her a definite 'no', and a hesitant 'no' which needed reassurance.

Mary stood by Jesus even at the worst and most painful time – when he hung on the cross. She was also among the first to see Jesus when he had risen from death.

To do today

If possible, give your Mum a hug today, and let both your Mum and your Dad know that you're fond of them.

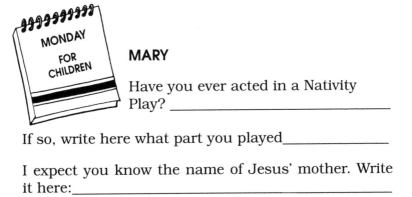

MARY

Have you ever acted in a Nativity Play? _____

If so, write here what part you played_____

I expect you know the name of Jesus' mother. Write it here:_____

On page 105 is a picture of Joseph and Mary with Jesus when he was a baby. Under it, draw a picture of you and your family.

Here are some things Mary gave Jesus when he was a baby. See if you can decode them:

1. JFIH

2. RIBMK QVMYYIFKD RILSEBQ   3. RTYYIBQ

Real letters:	A	B	C	D	E	F	G	H	I	J	K	L	M
Code letters:	M	A	R	Y	B	C	D	E	F	G	H	I	J

Real letters:	N	O	P	Q	R	S	T	U	V	W	X	Y	Z
Code letters:	K	L	N	O	P	Q	S	T	U	V	W	X	S

Your Mum probably gave you the same kind of things!

Now put into code a message thanking your Mum for three things you are glad she gives you.

What do you think Mary was like? When we read about her in the gospel she sounds kind and gentle, happy to do whatever God asked her to, brave, friendly and the sort of person you can trust. Jesus often told jokes in his stories when he was grown up, so he probably often made Joseph and Mary laugh when he was at home as a child.

When Jesus was your age he went to his school and sat on the floor with his friends learning a lot of things off by heart by chanting them. Perhaps his friends would come back home with him after school sometimes, and Mary might have given them all a drink of water, and a hunk of fresh warm bread each. Jesus' house must have smelt nicely of wood shavings, because Joseph was a carpenter. Jesus probably had a go at making things out of wood when he was quite young. Have you ever helped your Dad or Mum when they have been mending/making things?

To do today

Show Mum the key to the code, and help her decode your message. And don't forget to give your Dad and Mum a hug today!

THE DISCIPLES

Read Matthew 8:23-27

Much of Jesus' ministry was spent in the company of the twelve men he personally invited to follow him. They were certainly a mixed bag. Some of them we know more about than others. There was Simon Peter, for instance, physically strong and impulsive, though very timid in many ways. And his first reaction to recognising Jesus' power of goodness was to beg him: 'Go away from me, Lord! I am a sinful man.' One of the loveliest characteristics of Peter is that however many colossal blunders he makes, he is always prepared to change direction whole-heartedly once he realises his mistake. (Think of him during his calling; at his denial; at Joppa, for instance.) Jesus can use our weaknesses if we don't hug them to ourselves defensively.

Then there were the hot-headed brothers, James and John, who were so zealous in their love for Jesus that they were quite ready to call down fire from heaven on a village that didn't treat him well! But it was that same characteristic that made them throw themselves so enthusiastically into working with Jesus and learning from him. Jesus can take our natural characters and direct them so positively that they shine.

Thomas is so often thought of as the doubter, and this gives a very negative view of the man who spoke bravely when Jesus announced his intention to return to the dangers of Judaea: 'Let us all go with the Teacher, so that we may die with him!' It was Thomas' tremendous loyalty which was the flip side of his doubt about the resurrection; his loyalty to Jesus the man was for a while preventing him from seeing Jesus' divinity. Once the penny drops, his loyalty blossoms into powerful and unconditional faith, and he acknowledges Jesus as 'My Lord and my God!'

Jesus, then, was not choosing superhuman freaks or ready-made saints. Nor was he choosing the complacent. The one thing all the disciples had in common was that they all recognised their need of Jesus, and were prepared to change their lives in order to spend time with him. Jesus chose them, with all their irritating habits, their particular hang-ups, their different backgrounds and expectations. Gradually, through his presence among them, and then in them, he transformed them so their lives could shine with the healing love of God. And this, believe it or not, is what he will do with us, if we let him, however unpromising the raw material.

To do today

Imagine yourself in that boat during the storm. How do you feel when you notice that Jesus is asleep? How do you feel about Jesus and about your panic once Jesus has calmed the sea and wind? Now think of the storm as being a turbulant time in your life and go through the questions again.

TUESDAY
FOR
YOUNG
PEOPLE

THE DISCIPLES
Read Matthew 8:23-27

Perhaps some of you have been on a small boat when the weather has suddenly turned rough. At first it's just exciting, and everyone's screaming and laughing each time they get drenched with water. But if something goes wrong in these conditions, like the boat starting to leak badly, that's when you get really scared and it isn't so funny any more.

In our reading today the boat was pretty full, so she would already have been quite low in the water when the storm struck. Suddenly, from being a nice, peaceful voyage to the far side of the lake, this is turning into a disaster area, and panic sets in. You can imagine them all, with everyone shouting orders at everyone else, tempers getting frayed, the fisher-men among them getting irritated at the land-lubbers, perhaps, and water pouring in over the sides every time they dip into a wave.

And there in the middle of the boat they find Jesus, fast asleep! How would you have felt, do you think? I suspect I would feel quite annoyed with him, both for being able to sleep so calmly when I couldn't, and also for not noticing as we careered towards a possible early death. Evidently some of the disciples felt he ought to wake up and do something, so they woke him up. I don't know how, since the storm hadn't roused him – they probably had to shake him!

You can hear the panic in their voices. They're desperate, and beg him to save them. That sounds on the surface as if they have lots of faith in him, doesn't it? But Jesus obviously doesn't regard it as very strong faith at all. He is surprised they're even frightened. What does that tell us about Jesus? Well, I don't think it necessarily means that he expected them all to be immune from death at sea, or any other accidental death from natural causes. I think that, because he knew life here is only a tiny part of eternal life, he knew that we need not be frightened if we find ourselves approaching death, whatever our age when it happens, and however unexpectedly or suddenly it arrives. If we trust God, even dying won't cause us to panic.

The disciples Jesus chose were just a normal, varied bunch, who got frightened and made mistakes, just as we do. It was through spending time with Jesus that they began to learn what it was like to be free.

To do today

Look up Matthew 10:2-4 and from it write a list of the twelve men Jesus chose, both as his close friends and his students.

THE DISCIPLES

Disciples are people who are learning things, so you are a disciple of your teacher at school, your football trainer or your swimming coach. Hidden in this wordsearch are the names of the twelve people Jesus chose to be his students. See if you can find all twelve of Jesus' disciples.

The Twelve Apostles

A	D	T	H	O	M	A	S	M	C	E	W
L	S	E	M	A	J	R	P	A	Y	G	E
S	I	M	O	N	O	P	E	T	E	R	M
T	A	P	N	D	E	N	Y	T	G	S	E
W	H	I	B	R	X	O	F	H	B	A	L
S	K	A	L	E	O	M	A	E	H	D	O
P	V	J	D	W	J	I	Z	W	V	U	H
H	M	I	U	D	N	S	E	M	A	J	T
I	R	T	S	H	A	L	S	N	K	T	R
L	U	N	O	H	R	E	C	F	M	O	A
I	H	J	O	Q	F	B	U	G	P	Q	B
P	W	J	G	M	D	A	R	S	E	L	P

SIMON PETER

ANDREW

JAMES

JOHN

MATTHEW

THOMAS

JUDAS

PHILIP

BARTHOLEMEW

JAMES

SIMON

THADDAEUS

Jesus and his disciples spent a lot of time together, and they became good friends. I don't think some of them would ever have been friends with one another if Jesus hadn't brought them all together. That happens now, as well. I hope you are getting to be friends with other people of all ages on the Lent course. Perhaps you didn't know them before. Perhaps you didn't like them before!

If you have made some new friends then I am very happy, because Jesus has given you to them and them to you!

111

To do today

Here is a picture of Jesus calling some of his disciples, who were fishermen. When you have found the six hidden fish, colour the picture. You can read the story in Luke 5:1-11.

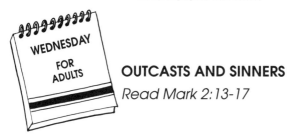

OUTCASTS AND SINNERS
Read Mark 2:13-17

I have mentioned before the danger of familiarity with gospel words dulling our perception. There is another danger of hearing the words since childhood in a church atmosphere. The danger is that expressions like 'outcasts' get clinically deodorised with one of those powerful disinfectants that kill all known household germs! In the context of the gospel, outcasts become quite decent, and very different in our minds from the gin-breathed alcoholic vomiting over the steps at a London station, or the glassy-eyed, sniffing drug addicts hanging desperately around the all-night chemist.

In reality, of course, these are just the kind of outcasts Jesus sought out, and to whom he ministered and brought hope. Surprising as it may seem, he loved them. It didn't matter to him whether they suffered as a result of misfortune or their own blundering or their own deliberate, selfish decisions. He did not come to them making pitying noises before going back to a hot shower and his own 'nice' people again.

Jesus was drawn to all the outcasts and sinners with a burning desire to make them better; to sort out the fundamental needs in them which had been buried for years, take away the self-destructive guilt, and restore self-confidence, hope and wholeness.

I wonder if you've ever noticed how Jesus never, ever, excuses sin. He never says platitudes like, 'Oh, don't worry, you might try doing a spot of fishing to take you mind off things!' or words to that effect. No,

Jesus knows they are full of sin, and he doesn't bury the guilt by excusing it – he eradicates it with forgiveness.

There are so many thousands of people in our world whose lives are restricted or even paralysed by a deep-seated need for forgiveness which is buried so far beneath the surface that it is often not even acknowledged. The contorted efforts to keep it buried result in broken marriages; damaged relationships; over-busy, frantic activity; illness; depression; despair.

In love, Jesus is drawn to each anguished outcast and sinner, now as then. He understands their real needs and can supply them. He still believes in them and longs to make them whole.

To do today

Think over those you know who desperately need God's love and forgiveness. Bring them with you to Jesus in your prayer today; don't talk a lot – just know Jesus is here, that he loves you and the person you have brought, and it is his pleasure to make them whole.

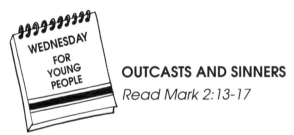

OUTCASTS AND SINNERS
Read Mark 2:13-17

Do you remember Zacchaeus – the short man who climbed a sycamore tree? Well, here's another of those despised collectors of Roman taxes, being picked out by Jesus and called to follow him as one of his disciples. Like Zacchaeus, Levi invites Jesus and his hangers-on to a meal. It seems there are a few gate-crashers, but no one appears to mind.

Except the Pharisees, that is. They are pretty horrified to find such an impressive, if unconventional, teacher sitting down to eat with such offensive company. Jesus is running the risk of being lumped together with the outcasts himself. It's true that some people will judge us by the company we keep. The outcasts obviously enjoyed Jesus' company, and many had started following him regularly. Why?

We are often drawn to people we feel understand us, and turned off by people we feel are judging us and finding we don't match up to their idea of what we should be. No one enjoys being made to feel inadequate, and everyone likes being loved and accepted for what they are, without having to pretend to be different.

That's the lovely thing about Jesus – we never have to pretend we're different when we're with him because he actually likes us the way we are. He enjoys our company; he even laughs at our jokes! When we're delighted about something, he shares the joy; when we slam the bedroom door and howl into the pillow, Jesus understands and sticks with us, even if our misery is caused by our own fault. It isn't that he's pretending we haven't done anything wrong. He's just letting us know that he loves us through the bad times as well as the good. And he'll give us the courage to put things right.

So that's why the outcasts loved being with Jesus: they knew, just by the way Jesus looked at them and talked with them, that they were loved and liked by HIM! And that was enough to start their lives changing.

To do today

Read Luke 7:36-50. It's a story about another out-cast, and the effect of Jesus' acceptance and forgiveness in her life. How do you think Simon the Pharisee felt about Jesus after this?

OUTCASTS AND SINNERS

Have you ever felt left out? Perhaps you have been playing with a few friends and suddenly you find they are ganging up against you, or not letting you into their secret. It's a miserable feeling, isn't it? And it happens to most of us from time to time.

Well, I have some very good news for you! There's one friend who will never, ever turn against you, and will always be there to comfort you. And that's Jesus.

God had always been known for comforting his friends when they needed it. Look at the next page and see if you can find out how God comforted Moses and Elijah.

Well done!

To do today

Jesus comforted a lot of people who felt left out and unloved. Read about one of them now. He's a leper, and most people would run away from him, because they were frightened of catching his illness. You can find the story in Luke 5:12-16.

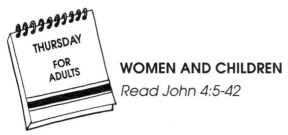

WOMEN AND CHILDREN
Read John 4:5-42

It's quite a long reading today, but a good one! We get a particularly informal picture of Jesus as he arrives, footsore, dusty and tired, and flops down at the well. His own physical thirst for a drink of water is the starting point for that beautiful teaching about Living Water. We then watch as the good news spreads before our eyes – the Samaritan woman is gradually led to faith and freedom, and then she witnesses to her friends and neighbours until many believe for themselves and are made whole.

We can tell from the disciples' reaction when they came back from the town, that Jesus was breaking all protocol by talking with the Samaritan woman like this – and the two of them are obviously wrapped up in their conversation. But something tells the disciples to keep their hearts open and their mouths shut. I think perhaps they are learning!

It is clear from the gospels that Jesus' attitude to women was remarkably liberated. A group of women were among his close followers; Luke suggests that they were people who had been healed by him and now accompanied him. Some, such as Joanna, were locally well-known – Joanna's husband, Chuza, was an officer at Herod's court. Some of the women used their own resources to provide for Jesus and the disciples; this too was quite an unconventional way of doing things.

To Jesus they were all 'family'. Do you remember when the disciples once told Jesus that his mother and brothers were outside? Jesus replied, in effect, that his mother and brothers were not just outside but all round him, too, because, as far as he was concerned, his family (and God's family) included everyone who did God's will.

We find the same closeness and family affection in the way Jesus welcomes the children. He listens to their pieces of news with as much care and interest as he listens to Jairus, the official at the local synagogue. There's no height, age or sex barrier blocking anyone off from Jesus. To him, each person is a special delight, made in God's likeness and loved with affection.

To do today

We often listen to people with half our mind on what is going on outside, where we have to be next, or what we forgot to do earlier on. Or else we tend to hog the conversation. Today, give other people your complete attention when they talk to you, and if you are usually the talkative one, ask them a question about themselves and really listen to their answer.

WOMEN AND CHILDREN
Read John 4:5-42

If you had been walking for miles in the hot sun on a dusty track, you would think it quite natural to flop down beside the nearest well and ask for a drink of water from the first person who came along with a water jar. So would I. But in Jesus' time, it just wasn't done for a Jewish man to ask a Samaritan woman for a drink. They wouldn't dream of using the same cup, even. No wonder the woman is amazed.

We never find out if Jesus actually got his drink, because instead he sees in the woman's eyes a great need, a great thirst to be loved and understood. She seems to be someone who is always hoping that the next relationship really will be all she dreams of, and as she gets older collects a trail of disappointment, disillusion and resentment like a chain behind her.

Compared with ordinary physical thirst, her emotional thirst for deep meaning in her life is painful, and Jesus knows that he can offer her God's spring of living water which will satisfy her thirst for ever. He begins by showing his respect for her by talking to her directly and honestly. As a result of their conversation, the woman finds the freedom and refreshment of drinking 'living water' and brings many others to know it too.

Jesus broke down barriers wherever he went. He treated women, men and children all as individual persons, all with much to offer, and all lovable. It didn't matter to him what people said about this behind his back. It didn't put him off if they jumped to the wrong conclusions or if he lost some followers in the process. God loves us in this way, so it is Jesus' nature to love this way too, whether it fits in with current fashions or not.

To do today

As you go about today, look at the way people treat one another. Notice who acts as if the other person is important and valued, and who acts as if the other person isn't worth much at all.

WOMEN AND CHILDREN

What do you think this boy is telling Jesus?

What do you think Jesus is saying to the boy?

Write it in the speech bubbles.

Jesus and that boy worked together to feed 5000 people! Jesus and you can work together to make the world a better, happier place.

Jesus likes being with children. He likes hearing your news and your songs. He likes to see you enjoying God's world, cheering people up, making things and mending things. He is very happy when you chat to him about everything.

To do today

Is there a place near where you live that could be cleaned up and made nicer? Perhaps there are cans left around that you could collect and recycle, or rubbish that needs gathering up and throwing away. Think about it and keep your eyes open. See if today you can leave a bit of God's world better than you found it. Then you and Jesus will be working together in a team.

THE PHARISEES
Read Mark 3:1-6

Have you noticed how often there are Pharisees hovering around whenever Jesus is working? For much of his ministry they accompany him, partly to keep an eye on him and check that things don't get out of hand. Some of the Pharisees were clearly impressed by his teaching, and some, such as Simon, invited Jesus to a meal. Considering themselves guardians of the true faith, they were being conscientious in picking Jesus up on the points of Law he seemed to be breaking. The sad thing was that although they knew the letter of God's Law off by heart, inside out and back to front, they hadn't really grasped the spirit of it, and so in one sense they didn't know the Law at all.

Jesus would not have considered that an impassable barrier, any more than he considered any sin or short-sightedness a barrier. But it did need healing if they were going to be able to accept God's saving love in their lives. So, time and again, we find Jesus talking with them in words of scripture that they may understand – talking within their frame of reference. He shows them how the scriptures declare the mercy, compassion, and loyal love of God, so as to remove their reading glasses, so to speak, and give them binoculars!

Of all the people Jesus meets, the Pharisees rouse him most to a mixture of anger and deep sorrow. After all, here are the people who should be in the very best position to be rejoicing at what is happening – the fulfilment of the scriptures; God visiting his people. And yet here they are swapping their glorious birthright for a stew of hard, undersoaked rules.

Near the end of Jesus' ministry we find his contacts with the Pharisees increasingly confrontational. He is not one to mince his words, and calls them a nest of vipers, and whitened sepulchres full of dead bones. When the man born blind is given his sight, Jesus' words to the Pharisees are particularly sad: 'If you were blind, then you would not be guilty; but since you claim that you can see, this means you are still guilty.' Jesus knew he had the power and the will to make them better, to set them free so that they could bask in God's love; but unless they acknowledged their need, as the blind man had done, his hands were tied and he could do nothing to help them.

What a delight it must have been when, years later on the Damascus road, Saul the Pharisee surrendered and allowed his Lord to take him over! The power of that experience did actually blind Paul (Saul) physically for a few days; the power of his subsequent ministry is even now reverberating.

To do today

Remembering that Paul was a Pharisee, read over the story of his conversion. Don't think of the voice as being an anonymous ghost – it is the same Jesus we've just been listening to. Read Paul's own account that he gave when on trial. It's in Acts 26:4-18.

THE PHARISEES
Read Mark 3:1-6

Have you ever given in a piece of work written from your heart, and had it back with just some picky comments about your spelling and handwriting? I hope not; it doesn't happen nearly as often now as it did. But when it does, you feel stamped on – because the teacher hasn't taken any notice of the important part of your work, the part that matters most.

That's the trouble with rules. They start out as practical ways of expressing what we value. For instance, if we want to keep a cricket pitch in good condition, it's a sensible rule to have no one squelching over it in muddy weather. But if the 'No one is allowed on the cricket pitch' rule carries on when there's no more cricket and everyone is squashed up on to the playground, it becomes a lifeless rule that needs adjusting. Or take the label on many medicines: 'Keep out of reach of children'. It's a very sensible rule which is designed to keep children safe. But if we followed the letter of it, rather than the spirit of it, we wouldn't be able to let children close enough to take the medicine!

If you glance through the book of Leviticus, you will find there are hundreds of very precise, clear rules given. They range from getting-rid-of-mildew-in-your-house rules, to which-winged-insects-you-are-allowed-to-eat rules. (It's only those that hop.) For a nomadic people, living in hot desert conditions, where food rapidly went off, and disease quickly spread, they are all very sensible rules.

But they are only God's Law in the fact that they

reflect his love and concern for his people in the conditions they find themselves – it is the spirit of caring love behind the rules which is the true Law of God. Some of the Pharisees had become so keen to keep God's Law pure, that they had lost sight of what his Law was really about. They were more concerned with the rules than with God.

In the story we have read today, the Pharisees are so hung up about the rule for not working on the Sabbath, that they view Jesus healing a withered arm as breaking the Law, rather than expressing their God's abundant love.

To do today

Look at this cartoon.

Proverbs 27:14
If a man loudly blesses his neighbour early in the morning, it will be taken as a curse.

On the next page, try drawing one yourself for the caption I've given, showing someone keeping the letter of the Law, but not the spirit of it.

Proverbs 25:20
Singing to a person who is depressed is like taking off his clothes on a cold day.

FRIDAY

FOR CHILDREN

THE PHARISEES

Do you know what the word SABBATH means?

It means:

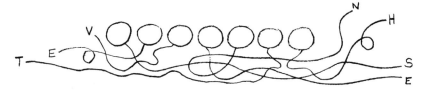

In the story of God making the world (Genesis 1) it says that God worked for six days and when he had finished he had a rest on the SEVENTH day.

In the ten commandments that God gave through Moses, he told his people to keep the SABBATH special, and not work on that day, so that they could remember they were God's people; it would be their day of rest as well as God's.

The Pharisees wanted to make sure that every bit of God's Law was kept. But they got rather carried away. They became a good deal too fussy about sticking to the rules, and not nearly bothered enough about what God wanted them to do.

Perhaps you have been in some houses which are SO neat and tidy that you're frightened to move and you don't feel welcome in them! Well, in a way, the Pharisees were like those houses.

When God told his people to rest on the Sabbath, he didn't mean they couldn't do good on that day. When Jesus healed the man's hand, he was not breaking God's Law – he was doing God's will.

To do today

MARK 3: 1-6

Why were the Pharisees angry at Jesus healing a man's paralysed hand?

RESEARCH DAY

See what you can find out about some of these close friends of Jesus:

St Paul   St Dunstan   St Monica
St Margaret (Queen of Scotland)
St Francis   St Martin   St Clare
Julian of Norwich

Bring any pictures and information with you to 'Together in Christ'.

RESEARCH DAY

*How would you fancy living in cramped conditions with the smell of garbage from the rubbish dumps all around and white maggots hatching out in your house? (This is how Sister Emanuelle lived for years.)

*Could you work happily among lepers and risk catching the deadly disease? (As Father Damien did, before leprosy was curable.)

*How about living in the slums of Calcutta and working among the filthy, the diseased and the dying? (Like Mother Teresa?)

This is how some recent friends of Jesus have spent and are spending their lives. See what you can find out about one of them:

Mother Teresa   Corrie ten Boom
Sister Emanuelle   Father Damien
Trevor Huddleston   Chad Varah

ACTIVITY DAY

Who do you think Jesus wants to mix with today?

*Tom's grandma?   *Lisa's Auntie?
*Rachel's cousin?   *Me?   *You?
He wants to mix with ALL OF US!!
Here is a good way to tell the others this.

You will need:

* a mirror   * glue
* a large sheet of paper   * felt tip pens
* scraps of coloured paper   * sticky tape
* scissors

Decorate the sheet of paper so that it looks something like this:

Stick the top of the paper along the top of the mirror with sticky tape. Then, when anyone obeys the message, they will find they are face to face with the person Jesus loves!

Bring it along to the 'Together in Christ' session.

TOGETHER IN CHRIST 4

Part 1
Everyone has a piece of paper and a pencil. Split into
pairs and everyone draws a portrait of his/her partner. (NB Don't panic – this is not an art class, and it
doesn't matter how brilliantly or otherwise you draw
– just make a valiant attempt and enjoy it!) As you
finish your works of art, share them with your partners.

Part 2
Stand in a circle. When you were drawing, you had
to look at your partners and notice them. Look now
at those on either side of you. Do you have to look
up or down to meet their eyes? Sing together one of
these songs which celebrate the fact that God made
us all different from one another – each of us is
unique!

> *Look all the world over* (Come and Praise)
> *If I were a butterfly* (OANA 214)
> *Thank you, Lord, for giving us life* (OANA 478)

Pray together for one another, and for our friends
and loved ones who are not with us at the moment.
Make this a time of open prayer; anyone who wishes
can pray aloud.

Part 3
The children bring what they were doing on
Saturday, and each child shares it with a group of
young people and adults. Then, in small mixed
groups, discuss these questions:

1. Between you, can you remember the names of all twelve disciples?
   (If you get totally stuck, find the list in Matthew 10:2-4)

2. Why do you think many of the outcasts wanted to be with Jesus?

3. In what way were the Pharisees blind?

4. Do you think church people behave like Pharisees sometimes? When?

5. Tell one another what you found out about the saints and friends of Jesus living in our time.

6. What have all these people got in common?

Part 4
Come together to praise God for the way he loves us; here are some ideas for hymns and choruses. Make it not just a great sing-song, but a great shout of thanks and praise!

Hosanna, hosanna (SOF4 42)
Jubilate everybody (OANA 274)
I've got that joy, joy, joy (Kids Praise Cassette)
At the name of Jesus (OANA 37)

and finish with a shared hug of peace.

WEEK FIVE
WHO CAN HE BE?

SOME SAY ELIJAH
Read 1 Kings 17:1-24

'Who do people say that I am?' Jesus asks his disciples. Naturally people were talking about him. You can't witness such healings and such teaching, or experience such rich feeding from so little, without wondering about the nature of this healer, teacher and feeder. There were other wandering teachers and miracle workers from time to time, but never anyone quite like this.

Perhaps you remember that in the first week of this course we were thinking about the way we make sense of life, and when a new experience crops up we have to shuffle our existing pattern to accommodate it. One way of doing this is by sifting through our filing system of past memories to see anything vaguely similar, slotting our new material in there. I remember my Grandfather, for instance, finishing up his first fruit yoghurt, and remarking that he preferred the ordinary sort of ice cream.

One of the past figures who springs to mind when the people are trying to make sense of Jesus, is Elijah. From today's reading you can see why; there are certainly similarities. This prophet, who had been living a hermit's life in the desert, makes a dramatic impact on everyone and they are all aware of the Lord's power working through him.

He shows, by ministering to foreigners, that God is Lord of all nations, and not only concerned with the people of Israel. Later he demonstrates that God is the real Lord of fertility, for he challenges the power of Baal, whose prophets are unable to bring fire to burn the sacrifice. Following Elijah's prayer, fire ignites the sacrifice and then a tremendous cloud-burst ends the fearful drought. God is the true source and sustainer of life.

Elijah is one of those seen talking with Jesus at the transfiguration. He must surely be one of those Jesus meant when he talked of past prophets long-ing to see the Kingdom of Heaven so close. Although a powerful, strong figure, Elijah is also shown to be very human and in need of his Lord's care. There is the time when, straight after the Baal episode, we find Elijah exhausted and depressed out in the desert, and God provides him with three great com-forts – sleep, refreshment and the quiet words of encouragement and hope. Jesus, too, had angels ministering to him after the temptations in the desert, and after the agony in Gethsemane.

It was Elijah many thought Jesus called on as he hung on the cross, and there were those in the crowd who half expected Elijah to come and save Jesus from death. We are often more ready to believe great things of past heroes than recognising God's power working among us in our own time.

To do today

Compare today's reading with Jesus' healing of Jairus' daughter (Luke 8:41-56).

Elijah heals the widow's son; Jesus heals Jairus' daughter	
Similarities	Differences

SOME SAY ELIJAH

Read 1 Kings 17:1-24

If you met someone who spoke at 70 mph and spent all his spare time peering through a telescope in his back garden, who would he remind you of? What if you met someone with protruding teeth, a big smile and a wicked sense of the ridiculous? When we're describing someone we've recently met, we might say, 'Well, he's a bit like Paul, with hair about as long as Wendy's and he does crazy things like Malcolm does.' Now we've got some idea of who this guy is. But it would be altogether different if we were saying we thought this new person was really someone else from the past. Everyone would think we were mad!

So what on earth was going on in Galilee if ordinary people were beginning to say that Jesus was really Elijah, a prophet who had lived hundreds of years before? Had their brains gone soft, or what?

The only possible explanation is that they realise Jesus is much more than a human healer and teacher. So who can be be? They search around in their memories and some of them come up with Elijah. Now there was a strange, powerful man who worked wonders and showed God's power. Perhaps Elijah was even capable of breaking through time to walk among them again now.

Believing this, they could settle the unsettling Jesus-question in their minds with an explanation that wasn't too mind-blowing. They already knew all about Elijah because they'd been brought up on stories about him. And if Jesus was really him, then they felt more in control.

As you can see from the reading today, Elijah and Jesus are like one another in some ways. Can you think of a time when Jesus brought a child back to life? Or a time when there wasn't enough food, but somehow enough was provided? Also, Elijah spoke God's word and told people God's will, even when it made him unpopular and put his life in danger. Jesus did this too.

In thinking of Jesus as Elijah, then, the people were getting close. They were recognising Jesus as a great prophet, a mouthpiece of God, and one through whom God worked powerfully.

To do today

Elijah was quite a traveller. Draw in his route after he left the widow and her son at Zarephath. Mount Carmel is where Elijah proved God to be Lord of fertility and life, rather than Baal.

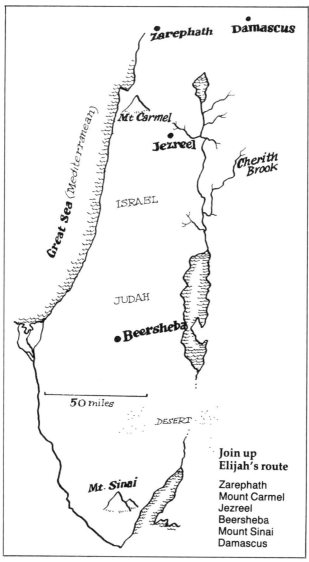

Great Sea (Mediterranean)

Zarephath

Damascus

Mt Carmel

Jezreel

Cherith Brook

ISRAEL

JUDAH

Beersheba

50 miles

DESERT

Mt. Sinai

Join up Elijah's route

Zarephath
Mount Carmel
Jezreel
Beersheba
Mount Sinai
Damascus

SOME SAY ELIJAH

Some of those who met Jesus thought he was Elijah. So today, we are going to find out who Elijah was.

Elijah was living about

Legs on a spider	Legs on a fly	Legs on a tomato

years before Jesus was born.

He helped people to know God better, and there are lots of stories about him in the Book of Kings in the Bible. Here is one of them.

One day, when there had been no rain for ages, food was hard to find. Elijah, feeling very hungry and thirsty, was just coming to the gate of a town called Zarephath when he saw a widow gathering firewood.

'Please bring me a drink of water,' he said, 'and some bread.'

'I'm afraid I haven't got any bread,' said the widow sadly. 'As a matter of fact I'm just collecting this bit of firewood to cook a last meal for me and my son. I've only got a drop of olive oil and a handful of flour left. When we've eaten that we shall starve to death.'

'Don't worry,' Elijah said to her. 'You go ahead and cook your meal. But first, make a little loaf for me. The Lord God will not let you starve – this what he is saying to you:

'Bowl will not run out of flour,
Jar will not run out of oil,
Before the day that I, the Lord,
Water the earth with rain.'

And you can always trust God to keep his word,' finished Elijah.

The widow felt she had nothing to lose by trying, at any rate. She looked at Elijah and felt sorry for him. If anything, he looked hungrier than she felt! So she went home with the firewood and instead of using up all her flour and oil at once, she took a little of it and made a small loaf for Elijah.

She took it to him while it was still warm, and it smelt delicious. The widow watched as Elijah ate, and he seemed to enjoy every mouthful; she was happy that she had helped him.

The strange thing was, when the widow took out enough oil and flour for herself and her son, she found there was still some left over! The widow invited Elijah to stay at her home, and every time she needed food, the widow found enough oil and flour for them all.

To do today

Another time, Elijah challenged the prophets of Baal to a competition. Whose God is powerful enough to send fire for the sacrifice? Baal's prophets pray like crazy but nothing happens. Here is a picture of Elijah praying – and look what God has done! Colour in the picture, making the flames really bright.

SOME SAY JOHN THE BAPTIST

Read Luke 3:1-20

John the Baptist was Jesus' cousin, and not long after he had baptised Jesus, he was arrested by Herod and subsequently beheaded. Seeing Jesus' ministry as a natural extension of John's, some people were saying that John the Baptist must be living again in Jesus.

As Luke tells us, people's hopes began to rise when they had first heard John preaching. They began to feel that great things were about to happen; there was a sense of urgency about getting yourself reconciled to God before it was too late. John, looking in many ways like the powerful figure of Elijah, strode out of the desert with a clear message that hit home to them: 'Get ready!'

Time and again in prophecies the Messiah – God's chosen one – had been promised. Could it be that here, in John, he had arrived? John must have got wind of what they were thinking because he makes a clear, public announcement that he himself is not the appointed one they are waiting for.

How easily John could have pocketed the glory at this point. There he is, with many crowds hanging on his every word, ready to acclaim him, and he directs their attention to look for another, who is so much more important that John feels himself unfit even to untie his sandals. It is a remarkable humility that we find in John the Baptist.

John's teaching is down-to-earth and very practical. When different groups of people come to him for advice, he looks at their lifestyle and suggests definite behaviour patterns that they can adopt. All his suggestions spring from the commandments: *Love God and Love your neighbour.* And all kinds of different people seem to have wanted to make an effort to change their ways.

John, since his conception, had been close to the Lord's will. In him the prophecies about the Messiah's forerunner come true. He directed the crowds at the Jordan, and he directs us, now, to Jesus. According to John's gospel, John the Baptist specifies Jesus as being the Lamb of God – the one he had been talking about as Messiah. According to Mark's gospel, Jesus' first teaching; 'Turn away from your sins and believe the Good News!' dovetails perfectly into what John has been saying about him, too. So there is much to make us think that John is right, and Jesus may well be the promised Messiah.

To do today

Imagine you are also among the crowds listening to John, and you ask him what you can do to prepare yourself for the coming of God's chosen one. What practical things in your life do you think he might suggest you need to change?

SOME SAY JOHN THE BAPTIST
Read Luke 3:1-20

As we saw yesterday, some people thought Jesus was Elijah. Others thought he was John the Baptist. Now John had spoken out against Herod, telling him he was wrong to have married his brother's wife, Herodias. This had annoyed Herod a lot. It didn't thrill Herodias much, either, as you can imagine. Herod had John arrested and thrown into prison. It was on Herod's birthday that Herodias saw her chance to get rid of John the Baptist. Her daughter was dancing for everyone as part of the birthday celebrations, and Herod, probably full of the birthday spirit in more ways than one, offered her anything she wanted. Herodias persuaded her daughter to ask for the head of John the Baptist on a dish!

Since Herod was sad to do this, it seems he was quite fond of John; perhaps he saw that he was honest and admired his bravery in speaking out. Anyway, he didn't feel he could get out of his promise, especially with Herodias to face, so he gave the command and John was beheaded.

According to Matthew's gospel, it was Herod himself who started the rumour of Jesus actually being John the Baptist come to life again. When you feel really guilty about something terrible you have done, it often stays around, haunting you. Herod obviously felt great guilt. Perhaps he half hoped that he hadn't been powerful enough to kill John off after all.

After John's death, his disciples took his body for burial, and went and told Jesus. The news clearly affected Jesus deeply, and his first reaction was to go off on his own across the lake. He and John would have know each other well all through child-hood, and Jesus knew that John had been powerfully used by God in preparing people for his own ministry.

In his grief we might expect Jesus to be irritated by finding that the crowds have run round the side of the lake and are waiting for him. But for Jesus, his grief if anything sharpens the love he feels for them all, and he sets to work, healing all those who are ill.

To do today

Think of the way Herod felt too scared to stand up for what he knew was right. What/who do you think made it extra hard for him? What things in our soci-ety make it hard for us to do what we know to be right?

SOME SAY JOHN THE BAPTIST

Some of those who met Jesus thought he was John the Baptist, so today, let's find out who John was and what he was doing.

First of all I will tell you that when Mary knew she was going to have Jesus, she went off to see her cousin, Elizabeth, who was also expecting a baby. Get a Bible and find Luke 1:37. You will need this to find the right answers.

Now help Mary to find Elizabeth by answering the questions correctly. You can look up the answers in your Bible if you want to.

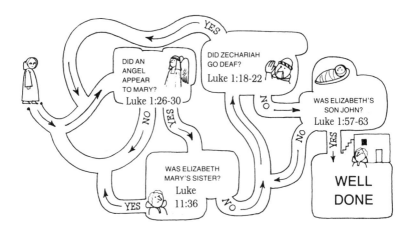

When John grew up, he started telling the people that they must hurry up and turn their backs on selfishness and unkindness, so as to be ready in time. 'Ready for what?' the people asked. John explained that soon the one God had promised would be coming. 'What can we do?' asked the people. John helped them to see which bits of their lives needed changing. And as a sign that they were 'washing' their lives, John dipped them all under the water of the river Jordan.

To do today

Here is a picture of John baptising people. Colour it in and, if you have been baptised, find out when it was and where it was.

SOME SAY A PROPHET

Read John 12:44-50

We often think of prophets as being those who fore-tell the future. But this is to miss out on the most important characteristic of prophecy, which is pro-claiming God's message – forth-telling rather than fore-telling. Sometimes this may well include a mes-sage about the future, but it can equally well elucidate the present and refer to the past.

In this sense we can see that Jesus certainly is a prophet. Wherever he goes, by word or action, he proclaims God's message of saving love, truth and direction. 'ı am the Way, the Truth and the Life,' he says, and he will stop at nothing, risking everything, to make God's message known. From healing Peter's mother-in-law to forgiving his torturers, Jesus' life makes God's will known and available; it is no longer hidden, or even veiled. From the parables of God's kingdom to the great, world-inverting Beatitudes; from the voice of authority calming the storm, to the weeping over Jerusalem, Jesus' voice is expressing God's thoughts.

Yes, he is a prophet, but even more than a prophet. Jesus not only proclaims God's word; he *is* God's Word. 'Whoever sees me,' says Jesus, 'sees also him who sent me.' This is what John was exploring and celebrating in the first chapter of his gospel: 'The Word became a human being and, full of grace and truth, lived among us.'

If we accept that Jesus is God's Word, however, the margins of our perception of him have to be pushed so far back that they fall off the page. We know that God is eternal, for instance. It follows that if Jesus is the Expression of God, he, too, must be always present, both at the unfolding of creation, and through every age. Here is a human, walking about in sandals, whom we are being asked to accept as being one with the almighty and eternal God.

No wonder that there were and are those who find this hard to accept, in spite of all the evidence; it demands great courage and trust to take on board. We may find we accept Jesus as Lord, and then still find doubts, so that we have regularly to take the step of confessing our faith. The truth is, indeed, enormous: that anyone of any time who lives in Jesus' company, will be enabled to hear and see that Word, full of grace and truth, because Jesus has promised to be with us always, right to the end of time and throughout eternity.

To do today

Read slowly through the Creed, not just as something the Church holds true, but as a personal statement of your faith.

SOME SAY A PROPHET

Read John 12:44-50

Q. What do you think of when I mention the word 'prophet'?

A. a) An elderly long-haired weirdo wearing sandwich boards and walking up and down the High Street ☐

b) What you get when you sell the bike you've been working on for months. ☐

c) The smiling weather people after the News, pointing to maps covered in raindrops and wind arrows. ☐

How did you do?

If you chose b) You'll find a welcome in the Society for Spelling Freaks. If you chose a) or c) You're on the right track; keep going.

Prophets are people who proclaim a message from God. It doesn't have to be a message about the future, it can just as well explain something about what's happening now. The message isn't always what we want to hear, because it isn't always God patting us on the back and telling us how brilliant we are.

When God speaks through one of his people it may be a word of encouragement and hope at a difficult time. That's like God putting his arm round us or lifting us up when we're feeling too weak to go on. It may be a word which helps things fall into place, so we can make sense of some event in our lives or in our society. It may be a word of warning, to prevent us from going further in the wrong direction, and to sharpen our pangs of conscience.

But whatever the words spoken, if it is a true prophet speaking, then the words s/he speaks will be given to her/him from God. Some of the prophets of the Old Testament you may have heard of already, such as Isaiah and Jonah, for instance.

You may remember the story of Jonah and the large fish which swallowed him. When he was asked to speak God's words of warning to his enemies, his first reaction was to beetle off as far as he could in the opposite direction! Another prophet, Jeremiah, didn't enjoy speaking God's word because it was such a dangerous occupation. But he found that if he tried to hold the words back, they burned inside him until he just had to tell God's will, whatever the consequences.

To do today

Use your Bible's contents page to find the names of the prophets in this wordsearch. There are 16 names to find.

H	B	H	A	I	A	S	I	R	U	H	N
O	A	O	H	P	O	L	C	D	I	A	W
S	C	B	J	M	L	V	A	G	H	G	H
E	H	A	A	F	E	N	E	U	A	G	A
A	J	D	N	K	I	K	M	O	I	A	I
D	O	I	O	E	K	D	T	Y	M	I	N
G	N	A	L	M	E	U	B	Q	E	S	A
C	A	H	E	D	Z	A	K	L	R	Q	H
X	H	F	J	O	E	L	R	A	E	B	P
M	I	C	A	H	I	J	W	Z	J	S	E
K	U	P	H	A	I	R	A	H	C	E	Z
H	M	A	L	A	C	H	I	M	Y	T	V

SOME SAY A PROPHET

Have you ever been asked to take a message to someone, perhaps to another classroom at school? Or perhaps at home to someone in your family?

Here are some messages with the words jumbled up – can you work out what they say?

* 'DINNER MUM IT'S TIME SAYS'

* 'WET IT'S TODAY PLAYTIME – STAY THE IN PLEASE CLASSROOM'

* 'SAYS WE DAD MUST MESS UP MADE CLEAR THE WE'VE'

* 'NANA'S HAD CAT HAS KITTENS – SAYS SHE HAVE WE ONE CAN!'

Tick the messages you would like to hear!

A PROPHET is someone who has a message. God gives the prophet the message, and then the prophet tells it to us. Sometimes the message is just what we like to hear, like this one: 'My people, do not be afraid; I will come to you and save you.' (Jeremiah 30:10,11)

Sometimes the message is just as important, but not what we want to hear! Like this one: 'I can see the wrong you are doing. Stop behaving so wickedly before it is too late.' (Jonah 1:2)

Sometimes God asks us to take a message or do a job for him. The job may be something we enjoy doing. Or it may be something we don't like doing. He never forces us to do it, though.

The trouble is, if we say 'no' we are stopping God from helping someone.

To do today

LISTEN TO THE ANGELS

Read Luke 2:8-18

If Jesus really is more than a fine human teacher and healer; if he is not a reincarnation of Elijah or John the Baptist; if he is greater than a prophet; if he is indeed the living Word of God – then we would expect to find eternity breaking into time around him. It would then be quite natural for the events of his birth to be somewhat unusual, and we would be half expecting the delight in heaven to spill out into our human perception.

This is exactly what happens. Whatever the precise details of the account of Jesus' birth, there is in the minds of all those involved, an unmistakable awareness of the presence of God directing and enabling, protecting and rejoicing all the way through. The joyous news of the incarnation explodes from heaven in the chorus of angels' praise, and the brilliant light of God's glory. This wasn't a secret message for the shepherds alone. It is clear that they told not only Mary and Joseph, but also anyone and everyone who would listen to them. Luke says that all who heard what they said were amazed.

So who did the angels proclaim Jesus to be? None other than the Christ – God's anointed Saviour who had been promised by the prophets. The shepherds are also given a sign, as a confirmation of the good news they have received: the baby will be in a manger. It had to be something out of the ordinary, so that it directs their feet to the right baby, and their hearts to accept God's Word.

Practical signs of confirmation are often given,

both throughout scripture and in our own lives, and I do not think it is either childish or simplistic to ask for them. (King Ahaz was reprimanded for *not* asking for one!) There are times when we sense that God is asking something of us, and yet we don't want to act unless we are completely sure of his will. At such times we can ask for a confirmation of his word for us, and then relax in his presence so that we recognise the confirmation with God-given wisdom when it comes.

The shepherds return from the manger dancing and singing their way through the dark Bethlehem streets. Their hearts are light, their joy is deep – they have seen their Saviour; God has kept his promise and visited his people as a human baby!

To do today

Are you still remembering to live expectantly each day? If things are looking ordinary again, take a leaf out of the shepherds' book: expect God to show his glory and enjoy it to the full.

THURSDAY
FOR
YOUNG
PEOPLE

LISTEN TO THE ANGELS
No Reading yet!

Over the last few days we've been looking at various claims people made about Jesus – some thought he was Elijah, some thought he was a prophet, and some thought he was John the Baptist, raised from death. Today we're going to join the shepherds on the hills outside Bethlehem and listen to the angels.

One problem for us is that angels and shepherds all seem to get tangled up in our minds with tinsel and crackers; Father Christmas who turns out to have a hefty support team of workers; over-full, tender stomachs and littered wrapping paper. Which of it is real, and which is just a nice little story that we're expected to grow out of?

You may find the question answers itself when we read Luke's account of Jesus' birth now, at the 'wrong' time of year. It's surprising how different it sounds without the Christmas spirit around!

Now read Luke 2:8-20

The shepherds react to the sudden brilliant light and the angel just as you would expect working men on their night shift to react – they're terrified! Wouldn't you be? The angel has to reassure them that this obvious power is not evil but good; once the shepherds are relaxed enough to listen, they are told astounding news.

They would all have been brought up on the hope that one day God would send someone as an everlasting king to save his people. This had been promised to King David about one thousand years before, and many of the prophets had talked of this Saviour – God's chosen one. What's more, they knew he would come from Bethlehem, which was known as David's city because that's where the great King David had been born and brought up as an ordinary shepherd.

And now here are some more ordinary shepherds, at Bethlehem, being the first to hear the good news; I suspect that set-up would appeal to King David! They are told quite clearly that the baby just born is the Christ – which means the anointed one of God. David had been anointed with oil as a sign that he

Afterwards they went in to Bethlehem and found that a baby HAD been born that day, and the baby WAS lying in a manger, just as the angel had said! So the shepherds knew for certain who Jesus was – and they sang and danced their way back to the fields that night, and told everyone the good news.

To do today

Colour in the dotty bits to find the shepherds' good news.

LISTEN TO THE ARMY OFFICER
Read Matthew 27:47-54

At Jesus' birth the sky had been pulsing with the brilliance and glory of God. As his death approaches, even natural light is darkened in an eclipse of the sun, and at his death the earth shakes and rocks split, expressing the literally earth-shattering event which is taking place. The army officer, watching everything – since he is on duty, and supposedly in charge of a routine execution – senses that in fact he is not in control at all; there is a far greater power in evidence here than he has ever experienced, and it is utterly terrifying.

Jesus had once been impressed by the faith of a Roman centurion. Now again it is a Roman soldier who grasps the devastating truth: Jesus really was the Son of God. And he's just been killed.

The full horror of what this means creeps over us like a cold sweat. If Jesus is the Son of God, we are like trees, putting the axe to our own roots; we have destroyed our only true source of hope; we have rejected all chance of salvation for ourselves. Seeing it all like this, through the eyes of those who had not yet witnessed the resurrection, helps us appreciate how many must have felt as they watched the body of Jesus being taken down from the cross that Friday. The appalling misery and emptiness washes over us still.

Throughout his life Jesus had shown consistently, by his love and care for people's wholeness, by his healing, teaching and transforming, that he was the Saviour, the Son of God. But the greatest sign and proof of this came after he was well and truly dead. It was when God raised his Son to new life that he showed us the meaning of all that had happened before.

Suddenly it is clear that Jesus had chosen to die; for otherwise we, as created beings, would never have been able to put him to death. His death must have been a free offering of love for us; rather than the crucifixion blocking off our chance of salvation, it was the act of salvation taking place. His death was not a ghastly defeat, but an earth-shattering victory!

So it is that we, who live after the resurrection, are in a position to see God's plan of salvation being accomplished. Jesus, once raised from the dead, is alive; he lives to set us free. He has proved himself to be both human and divine, so that we, with Thomas, can kneel at his feet in joy and say, 'My Lord and my God.'

To do today

Do just that – find a quiet place and time and kneel in joy before the Lord, who lives, and loves you, and saves you.

LISTEN TO THE ROMAN OFFICER
Read Matthew 27:45-54

Well, we're a long way from praising angels and shining glory in this reading. Instead we are plunged into the darkness and pain of torture, with Jesus' terrible cry, 'My God, my God, why did you abandon me?'

Crucifixion was a long, agonising death, so as to provide all onlookers with as clear a deterrent as possible. With all the pain of being nailed through wrists and feet, and the muscle strain from hanging in that position, the victim would find it increasingly difficult to breathe out properly. This means there would be a build up of carbon dioxide in the lungs, and eventual respiratory failure, causing death.

As the day wore on, the legs would sometimes be broken, so it was impossible to help breathing by pressing down on the small foot rest, and death would come sooner. But for Jesus, who had already undergone severe torture before crucifixion, this was found to be unnecessary. He was already dead.

The earth reacts violently with shaking tremors, and rocks split open. The Roman officer and his soldiers are terrified. This is turning out to be no ordinary execution. The destructive power of humanity seems weak in comparison with the greater power they sense around them. They begin to recognise that it is no ordinary person they have put to death. We can hear both fear and amazement in the officer's voice as he says, 'He really was the Son of God!'

But, Son of God or not, he is dead. His grieving, bewildered friends take him down from the cross and bury his body. They must have felt that they were also burying all their hopes and dreams for ever.

Then, on the third day, just as Jesus had foretold, everything changes. Death is unable to hold this Lord of life, and Jesus breaks that final barrier down. He experiences the worst that abandonment and death can throw at him, and remains forgiving and loving all the way into death's darkness and out into the fresh light of new, resurrection life. In doing so, Jesus opens a new trail that we can follow. He has opened up for us the track that leads to full life, and doesn't stop short where the body does. His new life shows him to be indeed the chosen one of God – a living friend and brother who knows and loves us and is also able to set our lives singing!

To do today

Spend some time today thinking over the fact that Jesus died so as to secure your freedom. And he did that because he loves you. Never mind what anyone else thinks of you – Jesus loves you!

> *I asked the Lord how much he loved me.*
> *He said, 'This much,'*
> *and stretched out his arms,*
> *and died for me.*

LISTEN TO THE ROMAN OFFICER

When Jesus was a baby, the shepherds were told by an angel that he was God's Son.

When Jesus died on the cross, there was a Roman soldier in charge of his men. Everyone was very frightened when they saw the sun go dark, and the earth shaking. The soldier realised then that Jesus was not just an ordinary prisoner. This is what he said:

Colour in the dotted shapes

And he was right!

We know for certain because of what happened on the first Easter Day.

Have a look at the picture on page 163. What has happened?

JESUS HAS RISEN FROM THE DEAD!

So now he is alive for ever and we know he is God's own Son who loves us very much indeed.

To do today

Colour in the picture and the words in good bright colours to celebrate the good news!

RESEARCH DAY

Either: Work through Mark's gospel, making a note of each person who recognises Jesus as God's Son, God's anointed one, or God's holy messenger.

Or: Read Isaiah 61:1-3 and make a note of how you think Jesus fulfilled this prophecy.

RESEARCH DAY

What do you reckon is happening here? Read 1 Samuel 16:1-13 to find out.

CHRISM   CHRIST

There is a connection between these two words – see if you can discover what it is. Why do you think Jesus is called Christ?

ACTIVITY DAY

You are going to make a model of that huge fish swallowing Jonah!

You will need:

* thin card   * string
* scissors   * sticky tape
* colouring pens

What to do:

1. Draw a big fish on a piece of thin card and colour him in as you like – he can be any shape of fish you want, but here is an idea of what he might look like:

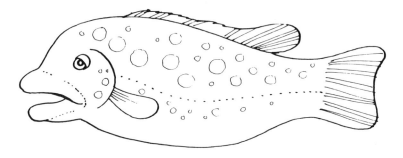

2. Cut him out and draw round him on another piece of card. Colour this fish to match, and cut him out too.
3. Stick or staple the fish round the edges, leaving the middle open.

4. Draw Jonah on to thin card, colour him in and cut him out.

5. Cut a piece of string about 30cm long and fasten one end to Jonah.

6. Tie a knot in the other end of the string and thread it through the fish from his mouth to his tail. Slot the very end of the string into the fish tail.

How to make your model work:

Unslot the end of the string from the fish tail. Now you can pull on it, and the fish will swallow Jonah. Hold the fish, head downwards. Squeeze his sides gently and he should drop Jonah out of his mouth again.

TOGETHER IN CHRIST 5

Part 1

Have one of your group as a narrator, one as Jesus, one as Peter, and everyone reading the rest of the passage.

All: A reading from Matthew 16:13-17.

Narrator: Jesus went to the territory near the town of Caesarea Philippi, where he asked his disciples,

Jesus: 'Who do people say the Son of Man is?'

All: 'Some say John the Baptist,'

Narrator: they answered.

All: 'Others say Elijah, while others say Jeremiah or some other prophet.'

Jesus: 'What about you?'

Narrator: he asked them.

Jesus: 'Who do you say that I am?

Narrator: Simon Peter answered,

Peter: 'You are the Messiah, the Son of the Living God.'
Jesus: 'Good for you, Simon son of John!'
Narrator: answered Jesus.
Jesus: 'For this truth did not come to you from any human being, but it was given to you directly by my Father in heaven.'
All: Thanks be to God.
Sing together a hymn or chorus to celebrate God's Lordship over our lives. Here are some suggestions:

> *How lovely on the mountains (Our God reigns)*
> (OANA 205)
> *He is Lord* (OANA 190)
> *Lord Jesus Christ* (OANA 302)

Part 2
This is an idea from Wild Goose, the Iona Community, and can be very helpful. Give everyone two pipe cleaners. Have a go at making these into some kind of shape that expresses the good news Jesus brings us. It can be very simple. When you have finished, find someone of another age group and give them your symbol, explaining to them what it is and what it means.

Part 3
In mixed groups, now, discuss these questions:

1. Look at the models the children have made, and try working them.
   What was Jonah supposed to be doing, instead of sailing to Spain?
2. What might put you off doing a job God has called you to?
3. What made some people think Jesus was Elijah?
4. What does the word 'Christ' mean?
5. How did Jesus show that he was the Christ?

Part 4

Come together in a circle, and pray for all whose lives are confused or empty; for those who lack joy and contentment; for all who do not know Christ's saving love.

Sing a hymn or chorus, such as:

> *Father God, I wonder how* (SOF 92)
> *Freely, freely* (OANA 150)
> *My song is love unknown* (OANA 337)

and finish with a shared hug of peace.

WEEK 6
WHAT MUST WE DO?

TURNING AROUND
Reading will come later

Peter has just been filled with God's Holy Spirit at Pentecost. He and the other disciples have had the most amazing experience of God breaking through into their lives and empowering them with his life. The noise of strong, rushing wind howling round one particular house in Jerusalem has brought all kinds of people to see what's going on – and since it's the feast of Pentecost there are many pilgrims and visitors in Jerusalem from other areas. Finding that each can understand the disciples in his/her own language, there is widespread confusion and amazement, with many minds filled with questions.

We are often more receptive to new ideas when our minds are in this questioning state, and Peter has a clear message he wants to get across to everyone, including us. Let's listen to him.

Read Acts 2:22-39

As we have been finding throughout this course, Jesus' offer of freedom, whether from paralysis, fear, sin, blindness, or anything else, always comes hand in hand with our desire to be changed. If we refuse to allow ourselves to be made new, then we can never claim the freedom we are offered. It's the same if we go insisting to God and to ourselves that we don't need changing. Since our God is a God of love, he will *never* force us into accepting his will for us or his gifts to us.

So what if we find, like many of those listening to Peter, that the significance of Jesus being Lord and Saviour has just hit home? What must we do?

Like the lost son turning towards home, like the blind beggar walking over to Jesus, we need to turn ourselves around to face him, and this will mean turning our back on anything in our life that is an obstacle to our relationship with him. We can't half turn, or we'll end up walking in the wrong direction! We can't come with our arms full of what we can't live without, because that way we end up still facing what Jesus is asking us to turn away from!

Like diving, as C.S. Lewis would say, turning to face Jesus is really very simple, because all we need to do is to let go. Yet it feels very difficult, because most of us are loath to let go – we don't like the thought of losing control of our lives.

But if we remember that we are turning to Jesus, who understands us better than we understand ourselves, loves us unconditionally and longs for us to know complete joy and fulfilment, then whatever is keeping us from a close walk with him becomes worthless and insignificant, and we can leave it all in exchange for perfect freedom.

To do today

Do a stock-take on your life as it is at the moment – where your thoughts, time, money and energy are spent each day. Are you trying to stagger to Jesus with your arms full of unnecessary junk? Has anything else taken the place of God as the central core of your life? Make a deliberate choice to turn around and face Jesus, and tell him about it.

TURNING AROUND
Read Acts 2:36-39

When you see something in a shop which you'd really like to have, you probably glance at the price tag. When your friend has picked you up off the floor, you have a straight choice – either you can leave it there and keep your cash, or you can blow all your paper-round and birthday money that you had been saving for something else, and become a customer!

Whichever you choose, you will be weighing up in your mind how important it is to you to have this wonderful garment/machine/animal. The more important it is to you, the more you will be prepared to pay, and the less important all the other spending ideas seem.

It's just the same with our lives. The 'price tag' on possessing Jesus and the joy of freedom is high. It will cost us all we normally 'spend' in time, money and energy on such things as selfishness, destructive behaviour, self-indulgence, and resentment. But the value of what we receive far exceeds what we spend: complete inner peace and joy which isn't dependent on 'lucky circumstances'; a capacity for loving which was previously impossible with our existing RAM; and the freedom to be our true selves.

I'm not suggesting that all this will come immediately, and that having got rid of your resentment now, you won't ever find it rearing its ugly head again. Turning our lives around is not a once-and-for-all transformation, though it can often be blessed with beautiful immediate results to encourage us.

But it continues and deepens and grows, so there is always more to come, and always a fresh sense of wonder at just what God manages to do with the material we bring!

To do today

Take a straight, honest look at your life and work out which things and people occupy your mind, your heart and your wallet. Work out which things in your life you are ashamed of and have perhaps been pretending you are proud of. Gather up all the garbage and mess you find, and bring it to the foot of Jesus' cross. His love in dying for you is what disposes of all that and replaces the space it took up with the joy of being forgiven.

TURNING AROUND

If you fall down when you're playing, what do you do? You get up again! Sometimes in our life we are being very kind and loving and then we're suddenly unkind and spiteful to someone. That's like falling down, as well. See if you can remember falling down in any of these ways. I certainly have!

Stealing   Swearing   Being Greedy

Lying   Being Lazy   Cheating

Being Rude   Being Proud   Fighting

We all fall down like this sometimes, so it's a good idea to know how to get up again. How DO you get up again?

1. Tell _ _ _ _ _ you are _ _ _ _ _ and would like to put things _ _ _ _ _ .

        SORRY   RIGHT   JESUS

2. _ _ _ _ _ Jesus for the way he _ _ _ _ _ you and _ _ _ _ _ _ _ _ you.

        FORGIVES   THANK   LOVES

3. Put things _ _ _ _ _ with the _ _ _ _ _ _ or

people you have _ _ _ _ .

HURT   PERSON   RIGHT

To do today

Colour the pattern so that you can say the prayer.

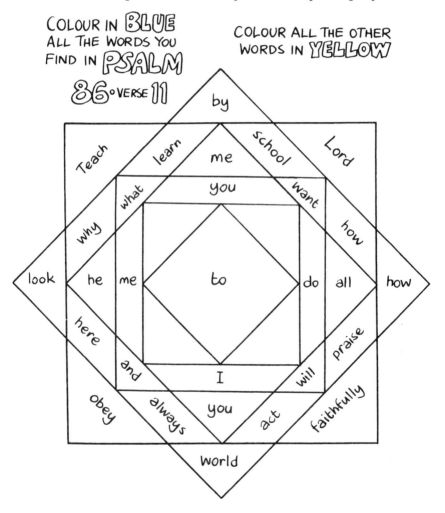

COLOUR IN BLUE ALL THE WORDS YOU FIND IN PSALM 86·VERSE 11

COLOUR ALL THE OTHER WORDS IN YELLOW

BEING MADE NEW

Read Colossians 3:1-17

Embarking on a new life in Christ is a bit like enrolling on a complete rehabilitation course. As Jesus said to Nicodemus, it's as drastic as being born all over again. Living IN Christ, rather than nodding in his direction from time to time, is going to transform us over the years to become more and more like him.

But what we need to be very clear about from the outset, is that Christ does the transforming, not us. That means that all the glory for our improvements will belong to God. So we can enjoy seeing them as they happen without thinking we're boasting; and we don't have to work ourselves into a grim frenzy trying to get our spiritual house gleaming before we let the cleaning team in.

Our transforming is only going to happen when we stop thinking and worrying about it, and spend our time consciously in the company of Christ. You know how owners look like their pets? And you know how we worry when our children get into bad company? At every level it's true that we start growing like those we spend time with. If we spend time with Jesus, he will transform us to be completely loving, full of inner peace, outward-looking and able to revel in the delights of this world as well as looking forward with anticipation to the world after death. And there are far more than 57 varieties of this species – every individual person will be gloriously different from everyone else. Just a glance at a garden shows us how much God loves a huge range of ways of being beautiful.

Our beauty may not be the kind of beauty the world raves about, of course. As God reminded Samuel, God looks not on outside appearances but on the heart. So it is from the heart that he will transform us, and that means we shall be beautiful in all kinds of odd shapes and misshapes.

Our culture badgers us into spending a lot of time thinking about our body shapes, and images. Living in Christ we shall find this pressure receding. Materialism all around us trains us to think possessively about everything; living in Christ we ·shall find ourselves being less bothered about acquiring and holding on to things. They just won't seem so important any more. In a society where we are valued in terms of how busy we are and how much money we make, we often miss the present by filling it with plans for the future and assessment of the past. Transformed in Christ, we shall find we are rediscovering the joy and freedom of living in the present.

To do today

Begin the habit of living in Christ's presence throughout the day. You don't have to talk to him all the time! Every time you remember, try thinking 'This is NOW and Christ is here.' Sometimes you will find this gets things in your life back in proportion; sometimes it prevents you from feeling crushed, and encourages you. That is because you have caught Christ in the act of healing and transforming you.

BEING MADE NEW

Read Colossians 3:12-17

When I see a chrysalis, looking all hard and dead, I sometimes wonder if the caterpillar has any idea about what's going on in there. It must be strange to be so drastically transformed – I've heard of mid-life crisis, but this is ridiculous.

In fact, of course, the changes take place very naturally, so that there is no one moment when the caterpillar has an identity crisis – at least, none of the butterflies I've talked to! And the way we are transformed is very similar. It happens naturally and gradually as the product, or fruit, of living in Christ.

We can't leap out of bed one morning determined to be humble by the end of the day, though many do try to organise their own fruits in this way. It's a mistake which happens from the very highest of motives – we want to do something positive to give to God, so we beaver away with our heads down, concocting the best new self we can think of, and then proudly present it to the Lord for his stamp of approval.

Sadly, it isn't the gift he wanted or asked for. And many get disheartened when they find they can't live up to the new ideal image they've made; they give up, convinced that God has let them down. Where did things go wrong?

We've got to be clay, not potters. We've got to allow God to do the moulding, transforming us from a squidgy lump, into the shape and style of pot he has invented us for. That way, our growth will happen smoothly, with each part being made strong enough to bear the next bit. You see, this potter already knows what kind of knocks and spills his pot is going to have to cope with, and he will build us perfectly suited to work in these conditions.

So leave the building to him. You just concentrate on praising him and being completely open, ready to be used. I know this works: I've seen the lives of hurt and damaged young people healed and bursting with new life. It's partly seeing their new happiness that made me want to write this book – the good news is too good to keep to myself!

To do today

Enjoy living in Jesus' company today. Thank him and praise him for making you new. Put up no barriers, and let your Lord start working on you, Lump of Clay!

BEING MADE NEW

First of all, have a look at these puzzles.

Can you change DOG into HAT in 3 stages, changing only one letter each time?

DOG

– – –

– – –

HAT

Answer: DOG, DOT, HOT, HAT.

178

How can you make this sad
old man into a happy boy?

Answer: Turn him upside down

We can get changed as well. We change for swimming. We change for bed. It isn't just our clothes
that change; I bet you have some adult friends of the
family, who look at you in amazement when they see
you and say, 'Good heavens, you HAVE grown!' They
don't seem to realise that growing is quite a common
habit among children!

When we spend our lives in Jesus' company, we
change too. His love will start to show through in us,
and we will become more and more like Jesus.

To do today

See if you can recognise any of these fruits of the
Spirit, either in yourself or in other people.

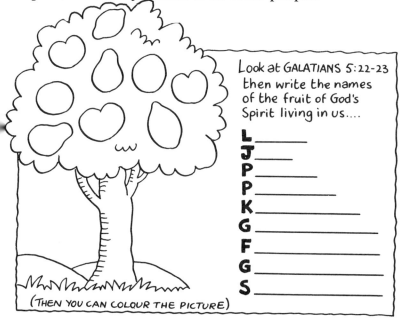

Look at GALATIANS 5:22-23
then write the names
of the fruit of God's
Spirit living in us....

L_____
J____
P____
P_____
K_____
G_____
F_____
G_____
S_____

(THEN YOU CAN COLOUR THE PICTURE)

FORGIVING
Read Matthew 18:21-35

The two great commandments which summarise God's Law, or Way, are interdependent; as Jesus said, 'in as much as you do this for the least of these, you do it to me.' It's impossible for us to say that we love God, and want to live in him, if we still haven't forgiven that woman down the road who said what I can't repeat and deliberately leaves her rubbish outside all week. Our life in Christ is being prevented from flourishing if we still have grievances hidden away which we may feel no one in their right mind would expect us to forgive.

One of the clearest distinguishing marks of a true follower of Christ is the capacity and willingness to forgive. This is one of those areas where Christ's teaching contrasts with the normal, expected behaviour of most law-abiding citizens. Normal, decent behaviour involves being pleasant, and forgiving up to a point. But it is generally considered quite acceptable – even honourable – to stop forgiving after a certain limit. It's as if we feel we will be lowering our moral standards if we go on forgiving indefinitely.

But now that we live in Christ, he is our only yardstick, and he says some outrageous things about forgiveness. He talks of forgiveness being not only acceptable, but essential in every possible circumstance. Yet surely, we start protesting, he can't include forgiving someone who assaults or murders your child? Or those who tortured your relatives or ancestors? Or those whose drinking and driving cost you the use of your legs?

In all these tragedies Jesus is there sharing the suffering of the victims. And as we saw with the woman taken in adultery, Jesus never pretends the evil doesn't exist, and neither must we. It's no good squashing our hurt and anger down below skin level, and thinking we have forgiven. That will only cripple us emotionally, or fester quietly and poison our loving from deep inside us, till we find that every relationship we touch is soured and bitter. Forgiving is often a long, laborious process, working through layer after layer of loathing we instinctively feel for those who hurt us and our loved ones.

We need help in tackling wounds this deep, and courage to face the fact that they are wounds – at first we will only know them as justifiable fury or distress, the responsibility for which rests entirely with the other person. The key to forgiveness is love. Impossible as it sounds to love those who have caused such pain, loving is the only way to forgive them, and forgiving them is the only way for us to be freed from the pain they have caused.

Happily, God is the Lord of love, and that means that he has limitless resources of the stuff at our disposal. It may be that when we first ask for his help we can offer only the desire to want to forgive – we may not at this stage even want to forgive, if we are honest. But it is an offering, and, as we saw with the feeding of the 5000, Jesus can do lots with a little. So offer him as much as you honestly can of forgiveness, and ask him to give you the love to enable you to forgive more.

Gradually you will find that your attitude towards the person is changing and Jesus' forgiving spirit inside you is allowing you to forgive whole-heartedly.

To do today

Begin work on this with God today.

FORGIVING

Read Matthew 18:21-35

Have you noticed how much easier it is to forgive someone you love than someone you dislike? It's almost as if, with an enemy, having something you can't forgive them for reinforces the fact that you were quite right to dislike them in the first place! And if we're in a group indulging in one of those 'What's-nasty-about-him/her' kind of gossip sessions, we've got our story to add to the pool of reasons we all can't stand him/her and are perfectly justified in continuing our dislike.

Now think of when someone you're really fond of does something to upset or anger you. At first you're furious with them, but gradually your affection for them starts making you feel like giving them another chance, making up with them or putting up with that part of them, all because you don't want the good relationship to end, and so you want to get rid of the barrier between you both as quickly as possible.

Jesus has a foolproof way of obliterating enemies. His weapon is more powerful than a rapid-fire automatic and it's guaranteed to work thoroughly and effectively every time. It's love. As you can see from our two examples above, the thing that makes forgiveness possible in the second case is love; the thing that prevents forgiveness in the first case is the absence of love. Where you have love, you get forgiveness, and where you have forgiveness, you obliterate your enemies!

So how do we go about changing our enemies into those we love, and can forgive? Well, as I said, it's Jesus who has stockpiles of this love-weapon, and one of the best ways to get a good bargain, as I'm sure you've discovered, is to go to the manufacturer's outlet and buy direct. Living in Christ means we're actually on the premises already, so to speak, and have unlimited access to this powerful weapon.

So feel free to use it! Use it lavishly and extravagantly because there will always be more available when you find supplies are running low. You and the God of love are in partnership now, and you're free to use whatever you need. Using the love-weapon is not a weak, weedy way of going on. It's a strong, positive way of enabling dramatic change in your relationships – with it you can change the loveless into the lovable.

To do today

Make a poster or placard with one of these slogans on it:

LOVE KILLS ENEMIES OFF FOR GOOD

LOVE – THE ULTIMATE WEAPON

LOVE YOUR ENEMIES INTO FRIENDS

WEDNESDAY
FOR
CHILDREN

FORGIVING

Peter asked Jesus how many times he had to forgive someone who wronged him. Jesus said:

59	37	69	74	93	38	42
x 8	x 12	x 5	x 6	x 7	x 9	x 13

USE A
CALCULATOR
IF YOU LIKE!

171	67	57	111	118
x 2	x 11	x 13	x 4	x 4

236	18.5	138	148	46.5
x 2	x 24	x 2.5	x 3	x 14

times! That's a lot of forgiving!

KEY	444	737	741	651	472	342	345	546
	E	I	M	N	S	T	V	Y

To do today

Read the story in Matthew 18:21-35 and when you next feel like NOT forgiving someone, REMEMBER!!!

SPREADING THE GOOD NEWS
Read Acts 4:8-31

When our first daughter was born, my normally self-controlled husband was out dancing in the rain on his way to phone our mothers with the good news! That's typical of what really good news does for us; many will still remember the exuberance of normally reserved people when peace was declared after the war.

We see it, too, in the shepherds at Bethlehem, and the disciples at Pentecost. Good news bursts out of us almost in spite of ourselves, and we want to share it with others. One of the loneliest times when we live alone is coming back into an empty house when we've been somewhere nice or done something exciting and there's no one there to share it with. It's part of our natural behaviour to want to spread any good news that has really had a strong impact on our lives.

If we have recent experience of Jesus making known his love for us in the way our life is changing, or our character, or the way things are working out for surprising good, then we shall find ourselves 'delighting' in God's love, and wanting others to experience it too. There are those who object to the word 'happiness' in connection with the good news of the gospel, feeling that this is a superficial feeling, and cuts off those who are not by nature 'happy' people. But I am sure that being a Christian really does gives us the light-hearted delight of happiness as well as a more slow-moving, deep-seated joy. The knowledge that we are loved, accepted, and delighted in, makes springs of sheer happiness bubble up inside us at the most surprising times and places, and when we see so many anxious, exhausted faces around, these feelings make us long to let others in on the secret of the good news we have discovered.

So it will largely be our behaviour – our friendliness, our loving, our happiness in surprising circumstances – that will be spreading good news to others. Seeing it may make some envious, which may in turn lead to persecution; but that's all right – Jesus promised us that as proof that we're doing his will. Some will see our reflected light and be guided to the source of the light, the God of love himself.

To do today

It isn't always easy to speak out in the face of criticism, ridicule or disapproval. But remember you're not on your own any more – it is the Spirit of Jesus in you speaking out, so you'll be given the right words or actions. Make the prayer of the wary disciples your own today. (Acts 4:24-30)

SPREADING THE GOOD NEWS

Read Acts 4:8-31

Even if the good news you want to spread is the best thing since the wheel, you won't always find a receptive audience, and you may well find yourself in a very dangerous position. Active Christianity probably ought to carry a government health warning! At the time of writing, Terry Waite is still held hostage as a result of active Christian service; a few years ago the priest, Oscar Romero, was shot dead at his altar in a church in El Salvador for active Christian service; many are held prisoner and tortured in various countries because they have been accused of spreading the Christian faith. There are many thousands who witness to the good news each day in their behaviour, and receive teasing, humiliation or rejection as a result.

So spreading the good news is never likely to be a cushy number, and should only be attempted by those who feel that spreading the news is more important than their own personal safety.

Taking a leaf out of your Saviour's book, always start by loving those you want to spread the good news to. This will ensure that you respect their present opinions and beliefs, and don't end up spreading a message of aggression and rejection under the wrapping of love, which would be disastrous and totally counter-productive.

In a sense, the best way to spread the good news is to BE the good news. When people see you happier and more confident, more understanding and willing to help without any rewards in the offing, you will start them thinking – especially if they knew you before! 'It must be something special if it's able to change him/her like that!' they'll say. They will be right. It is.

If and when they remark on anything in you that the Lord has done, take a deep breath and tell them. At first they'll probably think you're crazy or a freak, but you will have been seed-planting. Don't forget to pray for them regularly as well. After a while you may be surprised how quite unexpected people will seek you out to talk over all kinds of things, once they know you follow Christ. Just be yourself, and let the Lord use your voice, your expressions and so on; he will work simultaneously in you and them to get the good news spread.

To do today

Start praying for a particular person who you would love to share the good news with, but who is, at the moment, very sceptical about it all.

SPREADING THE GOOD NEWS

After the disciples had been filled with the Holy Spirit at Pentecost, they told everyone about the good news – 'God has sent his Son to set our lives free. His name is Jesus, and he was put to death on a cross. But God raised him to new life. So now he is alive for ever, and if you let him, he will fill your life with love, peace and joy!'

Lots and lots of people liked the thought of having a new life filled with love, peace and joy, so they joined the disciples and found that what they said was true. Everywhere, sad people were finding happiness, and ill people were being made better, all through the living power of Jesus. Then these people would run off and tell their friends, so that more and more people followed the Way of Jesus, the Christ. Soon they started being called Christians, and what people noticed most about these Christians was the way they loved one another.

If we live with Christ each day of our life, people will start to notice that we are different, too. They will see that we care for others with love; they will see that we forgive other people quickly, and that we are friendly and encouraging. They will see that living in Jesus is making us very happy. So we will be spreading the good news about Jesus' love by showing it in action!

To do today

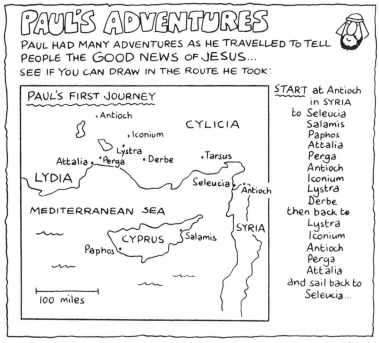

PAUL'S ADVENTURES

PAUL HAD MANY ADVENTURES AS HE TRAVELLED TO TELL PEOPLE THE GOOD NEWS OF JESUS...
SEE IF YOU CAN DRAW IN THE ROUTE HE TOOK:

PAUL'S FIRST JOURNEY

Antioch
CYLICIA
Iconium
Lystra
Attalia   Perga   Derbe
Tarsus
LYDIA
Seleucia   Antioch
MEDITERRANEAN SEA
SYRIA
CYPRUS   Salamis
Paphos

100 miles

START at Antioch
in SYRIA
to Seleucia
Salamis
Paphos
Attalia
Perga
Antioch
Iconium
Lystra
Derbe
then back to
Lystra
Iconium
Antioch
Perga
Attalia
and sail back to
Seleucia...

Acts 13 & 14

LIVING THE KINGDOM
Read Romans 8:31-39

I chose this reading for today because it seems to sum up much of what we have been exploring throughout this course. That encounter with Jesus on the road to Damascus had taken Paul by storm. It showed him the truth that Jesus of Nazareth, whom Paul had considered a blasphemer, and an insult to God, was none other than God's own Son. Since Paul had been actively persecuting Jesus (through persecuting his followers), he was overwhelmed with the fact that Jesus forgave him everything without reservation, even entrusting the spread of the gospel to one who, Paul felt, deserved total rejection, rather than this generous, loving acceptance.

So for Paul, and for every one of us, the realisation that Jesus personally calls us, accepts and forgives us, changes our whole outlook on life. Death shifts from being the final point of our existence, to being a gate, somewhere along the line, into the next phase of life which lasts for ever. That means that death and the ageing process lose their fear. Christ taking over our life changes our perception of what is truly important, and what is not; what is beautiful and what is not; what is treasure and what is not.

If God is for us, then we know that everything will be well, and we shall not be so disturbed by the constant anxieties and traumas of this world, or its uncertainties. We have, in effect, moved house to live as citizens in the kingdom of heaven, and can already live the forgiving, loving, compassionate, joyful way that Jesus described in the parables. We don't have to wait until after death to do this, because we can live in Christ *now* as well as later.

In the example of the saints we can see what we are all called to. The beauty and exuberant joy of their lives is not the result of any particular gene or talent. It is the result of them flinging open the shutters of their inner selves so that the light of God's love can pour in. From small beginnings, the God of power has worked wonders in them.

He can work wonders in us too, but only in proportion to the extent we open up to receive his life-giving power. As we drink him, feed on him and breathe him, relinquishing our possessiveness, selfishness and defensiveness, Jesus Christ, the living Word of God, will transform us. He will do this for the glory of God, and the immense good of the world.

To do today

You know the famous Holman Hunt picture – 'The Light of the World'? Imagine yourself on the inside, behind that door, and hear Jesus standing at your door knocking. Open the door and let Jesus, the Light of the world, walk into your self and give you the light of his constant presence.

LIVING THE KINGDOM
Read Romans 8:31-39

During the war a lot of babies were conceived while their fathers were home on leave. That meant that often the babies would be born and live for a year or two without meeting their Dads. Their Mums would talk to them about Dad, and there were photos around, but when the Dads eventually came home, many toddlers were surprised to find that Dad was a real live huggy person who loved them! We are like those toddlers when we meet Jesus for real after hearing him talked about for years – it changes 'I think' or 'I wonder' into 'I know!'

Having met him personally on the road to Damascus, Paul knows for certain that Jesus is God's Son – raised from death and alive for ever. He knows because he has felt Jesus' real presence enveloping him, seen the brilliance of his glory and heard his words of forgiveness and call to action. It may well be that you have had an experience while you have been worshipping in church, with a small group, or on your own, when you, too, have been aware of Jesus' presence in a very definite way. You realise, perhaps with surprise, how real and alive Jesus actually is, and it changes your life.

Suddenly the kingdom of God, that Jesus was always describing, is very close to you, and you can live as a citizen in that Kingdom straight away, alongside your earth-bound citizenship. It's a bit like setting off for another ordinary day at school knowing that you've just won first prize in a competition!

Living the Kingdom is the excitement of being at

one with the massive, creative power of God; it's the deep-seated joy and comfort of knowing that you're special and can treat everyone else as special, too. It's the privilege of being in a position to love and serve, no matter what insults are hurled at you; it's the wealth of having all God's resources of love at your disposal, to dish out liberally wherever you see it's needed. It's the pleasure of knowing you are living God's Way – the Way of Love.

To do today

Remember – you are a citizen of the kingdom of heaven; enjoy it to the full!

Living the Kingdom may be closer than you think! See if you can pick out which of these children are living the kingdom:

Now that you know Jesus loves you, and has lots of love for you to use, you can enjoy life even more!

To do today

CAN YOU HELP?

DRAW LINES FROM THE PROBLEM CIRCLES

TO THE HELPING SQUARES

ANOTHER'S
HELP
ONE
BURDENS
CARRY

[READ GALATIANS 6 v2.]

Unjumble the message

195

RESEARCH DAY

It's not so much research this week as a look at your own faith. Have a go at answering these two, very simple, but very important questions.

1. Why are you a Christian?

2. How is your life in Christ changing you?

You can write an answer in full, or in note form, but be honest and natural in what you say. You will not be asked to share the second question with anyone except God.

Bring a flower or some foliage to the 'Together in Christ' session.

RESEARCH DAY

Look in the local telephone directory to find out how many different Christian groups exist in your area. Have a look at one or two church notice boards. How far do you think they show the kind of warm, loving, life-changing Christianity we have been exploring during Lent? Do they look welcoming and friendly? Do they meet people where they're at?

Bring a flower or some foliage to the 'Together in Christ' session.

ACTIVITY DAY

You will need:

* a branch or strong twig

* a pot of earth

* thin card and scissors

* thread

* colouring pens

* your Bible

What you do:

1. Fix the branch firmly in the pot.

2. Look up Galatians 5:22 and 23 to find the fruits produced by the Spirit. There are nine of them.

3. Cut out nine different fruit shapes from card. Write the fruit of the Spirit on one side and decorate both sides.

4. Punch a hole in the top of each fruit and hang it from the 'tree' with thread.

Bring your tree to the 'Together in Christ' session. Bring a flower or some leaves as well.

TOGETHER IN CHRIST 6

Part 1
As you all gather, put the flowers and greenery in a vase which is in the centre of the room. Have the banners and placards displayed as well. Begin the session with a time of great thanks and praise to God for making you, and bringing you together and loving you. Have two or three of your favourite hymns or choruses which everyone enjoys singing, and sing with hearts as well as mouths, so it is a real outpouring of love for the Lord. Here are some suggestions for music, but do choose whatever best suits your group.

> *Thank you, Jesus* (SOF 500)
> *Thank you, Lord, for giving us life* (OANA 478)
> *Father, we adore you* (OANA 114)
> *Give me joy in my heart* (OANA 140)
> *Majesty, worship his majesty* (OANA 319)
> *I will enter his gates* (OANA 248)

If you wish, use your bodies as instruments of praise; feel free to move, and use clapping, shakers etc. to assist you in your praise of the God you love and adore. See how all the different flowers and leaves have made a bouquet; we, too, are an offering.

Part 2
In small mixed groups, discuss these questions:

1. What would you like visitors to notice about the people at your church?

2. How does Christ's life show in his followers? Look at the children's fruit trees for some ideas.

3. Are there any ways that different denominations of Christians could work together more effectively?

4. Why are you followers of Christ? (Let each person in the group share their thoughts in turn.)

5. In what ways do you sometimes find it difficult/embarrassing to be a Christian?

6. In what ways do you find that being a Christian helps you?

Part 3
You will need paper, pencils and scissors for this. In two's, mixed in age group, draw round each other's right hand, and cut the drawings out. On the hand, write your name, address, telephone number and favourite food. Now swap your hand with your partner. The two of you are prayer partners, and promise to pray for one another each day.

Part 4
Come together in a circle, holding hands, and use the Lord's Prayer, with silences in between each phrase, so there is really time to pray it, rather than just say it. Sing together a hymn or chorus such as:

Bind us together, Lord (OANA 47)
Shine, Jesus, shine (SOF4 110)
Spirit of the living God (OANA 460)

and finish with a shared hug of peace.

FOR ADULTS

SUGGESTIONS FOR HOLY WEEK

This week gives us an opportunity to walk with Jesus the way of the cross. Try to keep some time each day to be entirely with him. I know all too well how difficult this is, and sympathise with those who find little opportunity for quiet times in any part of the day! However, I will pass on a few ideas I have found helpful; perhaps they will be helpful for you, too.

Travelling times are often useful; using the 'This is NOW and Christ is here' realisation can put you into communion with the Lord without the need to say very much – or even think very much, which is essential if you're driving or cycling!

If you are a home-maker, chores like washing up and ironing are excellent prayer times. Use the physical work as the Eastern monks use the making of prayer baskets – offer the work as part of your offering of the present moment to be lived in fellowship with God himself. What better companionship for boring and mundane jobs!

Showering, bathing and washing are useful times, since they are, for the most part, fairly regular activities! Also, physical cleansing and refreshing remind us of the way Jesus cleanses and refreshes us spiritually. The shower of water can be a symbol of the outpouring of God's Spirit, enveloping us in the warmth of his love.

In other words, don't think of prayer times as being necessarily times of kneeling in church or beside your bed – if you find these more formal occasions are constantly being interrupted, look at every spot in your day when you're alone without too much mind-work to do. All these spots can become oases of prayer, which you will find very refreshing and calming. Spending extra time with the Lord this week will mean that the events of Good Friday and Easter Day will affect you more deeply than usual, and enable Christ to work in you, transforming you into his special you-shaped new creation.

SUGGESTIONS FOR HOLY WEEK

We've travelled quite a distance, spiritually, this Lent. Even if you haven't noticed any changes yet yourself, you have probably grown and developed more, day by day, into the new person God is making. Don't let all that growing stop because the course is finishing; a course is a bit like the push-off you give from the bar in a backstroke race, and it helps to get you going, but the real swimming you do right to the end of the race.

So use this Holy Week to stay very near to Jesus. Spend time in his company, and talk to him. Listen to his peace in the middle of muddle and confusion; feel his reassurance in anxious times; know his love for you when you find life difficult. Praise him and thank him for the ordinary and extraordinary things that happen through the week; and watch his crucifixion and see him risen, as one of his close friends and followers.

SUGGESTIONS FOR HOLY WEEK

You know how everyone has Advent calendars before Christmas? Well, let's be different and make a Holy Week calendar to take us towards Easter!

CALENDAR FOR HOLY WEEK

You will need:

* thin card
* pencils and pens
* scissors
* staples or sticky tape
* paper
* glue

How to make it:

1. Copy, trace or photocopy the pictures on pages 204 and 205 on to paper and stick them on thin card.

2. Colour in the pictures as carefully as you can.

3. Cut out window flaps to cover each picture

4. Tape the flaps on at the side of each picture.

5. Write the name of each day (MONDAY, TUESDAY, WEDNESDAY, MAUNDY THURSDAY, GOOD FRIDAY, HOLY SATURDAY, EASTER DAY) on the right flap.

Now you can open one window every day from now until Easter Day, when Jesus was raised to NEW LIFE!

HAPPY EASTER TO YOU!

Monday

Tuesday

Wednesday

Maundy Thursday

Good Friday

Holy Saturday

Easter Day